READY TO BE AN EDUCATIONAL LEADER

YOUR GUIDE FOR PASSING THE SLLA 6990

DR. DESIREE ALEXANDER

EduMatch
PUBLISHING

You should be aware of any laws which govern business transactions or other business practices in your country and state. Any reference to any person or business, whether living or dead, is purely coincidental.

ISBN: 978-1-953852-89-2

CONTENTS

INTRODUCTION
ABOUT THIS BOOK

After teaching test prep for the previous educational leadership test (**SLLA 6011**) and now the **SLLA 6990** for many years and seeing the success of so many educational leaders, I have been asked time and time again if there was a

recorded class and/or a book educators could purchase. Many years ago, I completed the online, self-paced class educators could enroll in to watch updated videos of the training (educatoralexander.teachable.com). I created Support Time where they could request one-on-one help and other systems that help them pass this test (educatoralexander.teachable.com). However, I was still asked for the online class in written format. Well, here it is!

This is not a stuffy test prep guide that is written in technical terms that puts you to sleep. I want this to read like a conversation between you and me. This book serves as a standalone guide with all the same information as the SLLA 6990 Test Prep online video courses, or as a companion to the online video courses to make note-taking easier.

The book is broken down into four parts:

- **Successful School Leadership Through the PSEL** (which gives background and an introduction to the SLLA 6990),
- **Logistics** (which gives a walkthrough and examples of the question types),
- **Multiple Choice** (which goes through most of the themes and topics you may encounter in this part of the test, specified throughout a dozen chapters), and
- **Constructed Response** (which provides guidance on how to formulate answers for this part of the test, as well as creating your own study guide).

The benefit of formatting the book in this way is you can jump directly to the part in which you need the most help, or you can read from cover to cover.

Lastly, do be aware that this book is meant as a workbook. So, highlight, annotate, and use this as a "living document" that you can add to, and consequently become your personalized study guide in preparation for the test.

Good luck studying! I know you will do great.

PART I

SUCCESSFUL SCHOOL LEADERSHIP THROUGH THE PSEL

1
INTRODUCING THE PSEL

$\mathcal{M}$y name is Dr. Desiree Alexander, and you may know me as "Educator Alexander" (www.educatoralexander.com).

Throughout this book, I'll be preparing you to take the SLLA 6990 Educational Leadership Certification, and this begins with an introduction to the PSEL.

This book is broken down into four parts, and at the end of each part, you'll see a **thinking activity** included at the end of the final chapter. Trying your hand at these activities will help you to understand each section more

thoroughly and give you more preparation to pass the test.

I hope you get a valuable experience from my textbook, and that it prepares you well for the SLLA 6990 Test. So, let's get started!

THE SLLA TEST

If you've gotten this far and you're reading this book, you're likely to already know what the SLLA test is. However, to clarify, **SLLA** stands for **School Leaders Licensure Assessment**, and this is a standardized way of testing if educators are ready to be an entry-level educational leader.

Essentially, the test measures whether entry-level educational leaders have the relevant knowledge that is deemed necessary for competent professional practice, measured against a set of standards (PSEL). The test is designed as an assessment for states to use as part of the licensure process. Several US states accept the SLLA test to allow a person to become a certified K-12 Educational Leader, including roles such as principals, assistant principals, district-level roles, and more.

The test is administered by **Educational Testing Service (ETS)** and was based on the **Interstate School Leaders Licensure Consortium (ISLLC)** standards, which were developed in 1996, revised in 2008, and then replaced in 2015 by the **Professional Standards for Educational Leaders (PSEL)**.

PSEL BACKGROUND

After a two-year development process between **The Council of Chief State School Officers (CCSSO)** and **The National Policy Board for Educational Administration (NPBEA)**, the new PSEL were approved.

After identifying gaps in the 2008 standards, CCSSO and NPBEA conducted research that recognized the needs of educational leaders and the leadership demands of the future. This process included the input of more than 1,000 school and district leaders through surveys and focus groups led by researchers. And so, after a lengthy process, the PSEL were born.

THE PURPOSE OF PSEL

The PSEL are foundational to all levels of educational leadership but apply particularly to the work of school campus leadership (principals and assistant principals). The **National Educational Leadership Preparation (NELP)** standards, which are specifically used in performance expectations for beginning-level building and district leaders (formerly known as the ELCC Standards) are aligned with PSEL as well.

However, the PSEL are used to define educational leadership in a broader sense. Overall, they are designed to recognize the central importance of human relationships, not only in leadership but also in teaching and student learning.

They have been specifically designed with educational leaders in mind, and the standards stress the importance of support and care that are required for students to excel, as well as the necessity of academic rigor. The standards recognize that human relationships are central to making the education system operate (for leading, teaching, and student learning).

Critically, the PSEL are "best-practice" professional standards that lay out the work, qualities, and values of effective educational leaders. The standards also communicate the expectations of this to practitioners, supporting institutions, professional associations, policymakers, and the public. The PSEL have been designed carefully to ensure that district and school leaders are able to improve student achievement and meet new, higher expectations. They are intended to help challenge the profession, professional associations, policymakers, institutions of higher education, and other organizations that support educational leaders and their development to strive for a better future.

2

THE 10 STANDARDS OF THE PSEL

*C*hapter One was an introduction to the PSEL, beginning with a brief background into how the ten PSEL were developed and why, as well as some background to the SLLA Test.

Throughout the rest of this chapter, each standard will be explored individually, along with practical steps to help you achieve these standards in your school. You can find a full list of PSEL with explanations under the resources at *www.educatoralexander.com/slla-test-prep.*

At the end of this chapter, there is a short thinking activity for you to try, as the end of this chapter also marks the end of this section of the book.

Try this first thinking activity before moving to Part Two of this book, which is all about logistics.

THE 10 PSEL

As you read through the ten PSEL, keep an eye out for the keywords that will help you to understand what each standard means.

Spend time highlighting any **key terms** or **phrases**, and make sure that you understand them before moving on to Parts Two, Three, and Four of this book as knowledge of the meaning of the important words will help you pass the test. And then come back to them often. These are the backbone of the entire test. Every test question is the manifestation of one of these standards. You do not need to know them verbatim (no question will ask you "which standard does this represent"). However, they cover EVERYTHING on this test, so why not know them as much as you can!

PSEL STANDARD 1

Effective educational leaders develop, advocate, and enact a shared **mission**, **vision**, and **core values** of high-quality education and academic success. You will notice that these initial keywords (highlighted in bold in this sentence) summarize this standard effectively.

It is not only the mission, vision, and core values that you want to see as a leader, but it's the *shared* mission, vision, and core values. In other words, this PSEL is about getting your **stakeholders** – i.e., your teachers, students, parents, community members, etc. — all involved in the process. This means not only developing the mission, vision, and core values, but advocating for them, implementing them, and evaluating them as a team.

The major question we must ask for this standard is this: As a school leader, how do you develop and facilitate the **implementation** of a shared mission, vision, and core values? You don't want to come up with a fluffy mission, vision, and values that don't really get to the core of your campus. That would be easy to do, but it is definitely best avoided!

Instead, you need your mission, vision, and core values to have actionable SMART goals you can actually achieve. So, asking yourself how you are going to implement a *shared* mission, vision, and core values is paramount to success and must be planned with foresight from the very beginning.

Your Core Values

This standard is most of all about how effective leaders must think about developing an educational mission for the school in order to promote the academic success and well-being of each student.

Think about how your school is represented in the community and how your school collaborates with your surrounding community. When considering this, think about how you use these answers to promote the school vision and further develop this vision.

Your focus is to articulate, advocate, and cultivate the **core values** of the school.

Avoid doing this in a haphazard way, as that would only cause you implementation problems down the line. You want to be able to look at your school and have your mission and vision align with how to best support your students, and this means deciding on what your core values are first.

In your core values, you should include core policy areas that address concerns, such as how you can support equity on campus and meet and deliver on high expectations.

Use these core policy areas as a starting point to develop your core values, and then you can open up a dialogue process from there to come to a final decision about what your core values should be.

Remember that knowing your core values leads to figuring out your mission and vision, so this is a vital step in the process. This means you should provide adequate time and thought for this.

Once you've carefully considered your core values, move on to deciding upon your mission before setting your vision.

Your Mission

To craft your school's mission, you need to look at how you can strategically develop, implement, and evaluate actions – not just push out fluff for the sake of it. And when I say you, I mean you and your stakeholders are making all of these decisions together. As a strong, effective leader, you make NO decisions by yourself. When you find your core values are effective and ready to be implemented, then it is time to carefully consider what your mission should be, which is a slightly different process.

A good way of considering what your mission should be is that it should be designed to demonstrate what your organization is doing in the here and now – *at this moment in time*.

Your mission needs to be relevant. It needs to be action-oriented. It should allow a person to understand your organization well, and also make them want to move; in other words, make them want to act. Think of it this way: a mission is about providing an exact purpose of why someone is part of the organization. It gives them that laser focus to get things done, by any means necessary!

When drafting your mission statement, think about that fundamental issue: ***What are we doing here***? This will become a main influence for your vision.

Your Vision

Your vision is the next and final step in the process after you have created your mission. It moves forward from your mission but is still reliant on those core values as the basis.

It sets out not what you're doing now, but where your mission will take you in the immediate future. It should lay the foundation for where you want to be in five years' time, setting up goals to be reached. Again, you don't want this vision to be fluffy; instead, you want it to be clear and have actionable goals. When setting up your vision, you don't want to come up with anything that sounds too heady and dreamy.

Remember that anything that slips into being too idealistic also becomes unachievable, which is demotivating. So, keep a clear focus on your vision.

Make sure your vision has **realistic** and **achievable** goals so that people feel they can accomplish it. This will then provide the motivation that is needed for staff to get out there and achieve your vision.

As you did with creating your mission, start from the beginning, and then have a long think about where you want your organization to be in five years.

Make your vision **specific**, and make it **actionable**. Without these two elements, any vision you create will be worthless. Therefore, it is extremely important that you set out a vision with clear goals that can be achieved within a set timeframe.

Perhaps you can see now why the previous step – creating a solid mission – is vital in all this, because your mission lays the basis for creating the vision.

Your core values influence your mission. All three elements of **mission**, **vision**, and **core values** go hand-in-hand.

Three Practical Steps to Success

Now, we'll put all of this into practice by demonstrating **three real-world examples** of things that you can do to get the ball rolling:

1. Verify that all your goals in your **vision**, **mission**, and **core values** are SMART goals. This means goals that are **Specific**, **Measurable**, **Achievable** (or action-oriented), **Realistic**, and **Timely**.

Next, make sure with every step of the way, you can actually **measure** what you're doing. Without any monitoring, it will be difficult to measure any progress, and without progress, how do you measure success?

Definitely make sure that all of your goals have a measurable outcome, in other words, something that you can track along the way.

The next part of this process is ensuring that every goal you create is action-oriented and can be achieved, and that is within a realistic timeframe.

If you follow the SMART goals framework, you should be able to create some solid mission, vision, and core values without any unwanted fluff. They will become goals that actually mean something for you and your organization, and something that staff can relate to and achieve.

2. Something else you can do is create a **committee of stakeholders**. This means banding together a group of knowledgeable people you can rely on to help you through important decision-making and actionable implementation.

Bear in mind that a stakeholder is literally anyone who has a stake in your school, so this includes teachers, students, parents, and community members. Anyone who has any stake in the success of your school could be eligible to form part of the committee.

Naturally, who you select to be part of the committee will depend on the nature of it, and also your preference, where individual members' experiences or proven track record could be considered.

3. A third technique you can put into practice is to create action steps to implement your **mission**, **vision**, and **core values**. This moves away from the SMART model as you get people to take control and go full steam ahead!

idea   planning   strategy   success

One key part of SMART goals is making them achievable, and this means making them action-oriented. Now is when you're really getting down to business and laying out the steps to answer: ***What exactly are the action steps?***

You now have your mission and vision, driven by your core goals, but the question now is how to get there? Creating actionable points and steps is *vital* in making your vision a reality.

This is not to say that once you create your actionable goals, they will be set in stone and remain unchanged for the next five years. You may find that you need to update them as regularly as per semester, which is why you need to follow the SMART principles and make any goals measurable so that you can track their progress.

Always bear in mind that every decision that you make on campus should be influenced by your core values, mission, and vision.

In other words, if you make a decision that is not guided by any of these three elements of core values, mission, and vision, or the decision doesn't fit in with them somehow, then this provides a good opportunity to stop what you're doing and really evaluate those decisions.

PSEL STANDARD 2

This standard is focused on **ethics** and **professional norms**. Effective educational leaders act ethically and adhere to professional norms.

To dig deeper into this, we should ask ourselves: As a school leader, what processes do you use to encourage individuals in the organization to act in an ethical manner and practice principles of a fair process?

First, those principles need to be identified. Next, you must consider what you are doing to encourage that those principles are acted upon ethically and fairly.

Keep in mind that the way to teach ethics is to primarily be ethical yourself and, therefore, lead by example. This may sound obvious, but sometimes even the most seemingly straightforward concepts are overlooked.

Lead by example and prove that the best way to *teach* ethics is to *model* ethics. Therefore, you need to consider what you are doing and what processes are in place to make sure that everyone on your campus is able to observe your ethical behavior. This means that effective leaders act ethically and professionally in everything they do. They act as role models, and their very existence is a teaching and learning process in itself.

Think about how this could manifest in your everyday interactions with staff and faculty. What are those key moments of relationship-building (but keep in mind that, first and foremost, those relationships ought to be professional and not personal)?

This is sometimes difficult to achieve in a personable profession such as the education sector. Still, as an educational leader, it is vital that you keep these relationships strictly professional.

When you become an educational leader, your relationship with others will change – because it has to. For example, if you become an educational leader on a campus where you had previously been a teacher, this has benefits and drawbacks.

The benefits might be that you already know the campus, the people, and the culture. But the drawbacks are more overbearing, as you would realize that you can't act the same way with other staff members as you did when you were a teacher and their peer. You won't be able to have those same conversations, nor go out for drinks every Friday. Your role will have changed – from colleague to leader. Of course, it would still be possible to maintain some friendships as a leader, it is just that you would have to appreciate that your role and position in the social structure have changed. This makes these kinds of interactions intrinsically different.

This may be a large leap, but you will have to do it as you transition from a colleague to a leader. You may have to have those hard conversations, which allow you to build relationships, yet remain professional. You must now adjust and accept that your role as a leader will change the dynamic of your role and your relationships on any campus (whether you are new to the campus/department or not). It's going to really help you as a leader if you establish those personal-professional boundaries early on and provide he transparency of ensuring everyone knows those boundaries.

Naturally, you always want to have transparency in everything you do. If someone asks you a question, you should be able to answer it, even if the answer is, "I'll get back to you on that." Make sure you mean it, act on it, and have a real reply to that individual.

Transparency allows people to see that you're not hiding anything, leaving them without any reason to suspect you of any wrongdoing. This will help to build trust and respect.

If you are treating people with fairness, there should also be no problem with being transparent. This includes responding to all questions asked. Again, even if it's something that you cannot answer fully, it is important that you still give them an answer.

If you don't answer questions asked of you, then it raises suspicion and heightens mistrust – both recipes for disaster. If you keep the communication channels open, and always attempt to provide an answer to any questions, even if not straight away or not a complete reply, this does wonders for building those relationships.

Furthermore, you must also show that you place children at the center of all decision-making. This is another method of leading by example, which also proves you are a worthy educational leader while simultaneously reminding everyone why they are there, even as this is performed inherently.

One of the most important aspects of ethical behavior is communication. You must ensure that what you want to do is not only communicated, but also the reason why you want to do it. This is why you do not make decisions on your own and always ask for stakeholder input.

You need to create a culture so that other people make the decisions with you, alongside you, and that your leadership is not a dictatorship. You will find that you get much better results if everything is transparent and everything is moral.

Three Practical Steps to Success

After reading the above, you would know that it is vital that as an educational leader, you must set boundaries, promote professional relationships, and lead by example in a way that demonstrates your ethics and morals.

Three real-world actions that you can do to start leading this standard are the following:

1. Create opportunities to review your climate and culture. The climate of the school/department is made up of the collective assumptions stakeholders have made about your school/department. The culture of your school/department is how your stakeholders feel about the environment of your school/department on a day-to-day basis. This is not just for you. It is also for your staff and gives you an opportunity to look around and consider what is not ethical on campus and to ask yourself why it is not ethical. You will find one of the hardest things for a leader is your perception versus reality.

So, if you are saying to yourself: "I am transparent; I am ethical," but no one else sees it that way, then it is your primary task to create the opportunities to discuss and eliminate any negative assumptions that exist. This action helps you reach the most effective way to communicate with your staff. Perception is reality, so if your reality is not matching everyone's else's perception, ignoring it or getting anger at it will not make this disconnect any better. All you can do is discuss it and create action steps to move forward as a team.

2. Consider what method of communication works best for your team. For example, you may consider completely changing habits like requesting all staff check email regularly.

However, adopting this method may not produce what is required. Your goal as an educational leader is to ensure that communication works and does not break down. Therefore, for the purpose of what you're trying to achieve, it would be better to work with what you have.

Instead of simply trying to change habits, a better way to approach this would be to adapt your method to meet the current climate until there is a better opportunity in the future to tackle the email  preference. Deal with the issue surrounding communication flow first; make sure it gets resolved, and then you can get back to changing habits at a later date.

3. You should create an ethics committee of adults and students. This committee should be composed of educators, parents, and students, and would serve as a check and balance to the ethics of campus.

The topics to be considered by this committee could include issues such as whether students are being equally punished or reprimanded in the same way, or otherwise generally promoting fairness on campus.

Having an ethics committee is actually an incredibly useful tool for an educational leader, as it provides insight as to what you may otherwise overlook. It provides you with an extremely

useful way of managing ethics and
morals.

PSEL STANDARD 3

This standard addresses **equity**
and **cultural responsiveness**. The purpose of this standard is
effective educational leaders ensuring equitable practices and
educational opportunities, as well as cultural responsive
practices that make certain each student's academic success and
well-being are duly promoted.

Hopefully, the issues of equity and cultural responsiveness are
already high on the agenda of every single school. The actions
you take here would just be about fine-tuning these practices.

However, you want to make sure that everyone understands –
both staff and students – what equity and cultural
responsiveness are.

Equity is different from equality. Put simply, equality essentially
means *"the same for all,"* whereas equity means *"the quality of
being fair and impartial."* There is a misconception that
everyone starts from the same place, so if we give everyone the
same thing to succeed, it is equal (equality). However, we know
that everyone does not start with the same resources. So, we
need to consider what we can do to help everyone individually
(equity).

When it comes to cultural responsiveness, look at how instruction is provided, or how it is demonstrated in human interactions. For a simplified definition, cultural responsiveness means understanding various cultures of your students and ensuring their culture is represented in the school, and that all decisions that are made consider culture, and connect to the culture of your stakeholders.

This means making sure that the lessons that you're teaching are relevant to each and every one of the students, that their culture is not denied, and that all cultures are included. All aspects of culture should be carefully considered and included.

When people say the word "culture," all too often, they automatically think of race and gender, but there are many other aspects to culture. These might include family origins, religion, or a plethora of other customs and backgrounds.

The main thing is to ensure your stakeholders' culture is being validated. This can be demonstrated in many facets of education, from the individual lessons that are being taught to the entire curriculum to the mission, vision, and core values of the entire school/district. The question that you never want to hear from a student is, "Why am I learning this," which could indicate some irrelevance to them in light of their cultural background. It is part of your responsibility to make sure that every lesson taught has cultural relevance to your students.

As a school leader, you need to address what practices, processes, and procedures are used to create an ethical and culturally responsive learning environment.

Understanding what equity is and acting equitably and not merely trying to reach equality is paramount. It is vital that you understand all your educators' and students' backgrounds and needs, guarantee that they are treated fairly, feel included, and view their diversity as an asset.

One way you can go about this is to ensure that your student policies address misconduct in unbiased ways, which is a big issue in schools. You want to make sure that the policies address matters of equity and act with cultural confidence.

Three Practical Steps to Success

After understanding what is meant by equity and cultural responsiveness, three real-world action examples are the following:

1. Create ways to learn more about the adults and the students, while maintaining your professionalism. Start discussions about equity and cultural responsiveness. Bring everyone into this discussion to get their views, which also highlights that all parties are involved in it together, and **everyone has a responsibility towards achieving equity and cultural responsiveness**.

· · ·

2. You should ensure that everyone (the adults and the students) on campus is aware of the difference between equity and equality, and more importantly, they are aware of what they should be doing to **strive for equity**. In other words, make sure that there is a process of implementing, monitoring and assessing the cultural responsiveness and equitable practices of your campus/department.

3. Finally, create an **equity committee** of adults and students. Similar to the previous committees that have been suggested, this could comprise teachers and students, but the focus here would be on reaching cultural responsiveness and equity. Bear in mind that perception is reality, and so having those dedicated people who can report back to tell you where your campus is thriving, or having them highlight areas that need improvement, is crucial.

PSEL STANDARD 4

Standard 4 deals with **curriculum instruction** and **assessment**. It focuses on how the curriculum is taught and how the learning elements are assessed.

Effective educational leaders develop and support an intellectually rigorous and coherent system of curriculum design, instruction methodology, and best-practice assessment in order to promote each student's academic success and well-being.

Therefore, the main question for this standard is centered on the term "rigor." So let's consider what is meant when we apply the word *rigor*.

A rigorous curriculum means that it is aligned to the state and national standards. This does not mean that the curriculum ought to be "hard" or especially "difficult."

Instruction should be engaging and the educational leader must ensure instruction is centered around making each lesson matter to the students. Every lesson that is taught ought to hold some significance to the students. Therefore, teachers should be getting their students involved in the lessons at every turn.

Effective leaders implement inherent systems of personal instruction and assessment, which, of course, promote your **mission**, **vision**, and **core values**.

Everything you do in school must promote these three crucial aspects, and if it doesn't, then that means something is either wrong with what you're doing or wrong with your **mission**, **vision**, and **core values**.

To ensure effective instruction is to promote your instructional practice to be student-centered. You want the learning environment to create a healthy sense of self for the students, with all of the aforementioned cultural responsiveness mixed in there. This creates the right balance and a positive learning experience.

The final part of this standard is about gathering the necessary assessment data to make the best decisions. Often, one of the key problems is that plenty of assessments are undertaken by  students, but the data is not ***aggregated*** by the teachers to inform the assessment correctly.

Aggregation is a word that is often misunderstood and used incorrectly. The best way of understanding it is that it is a way of "connecting the dots."

This means that aggregation is the process of looking at different metrics and then marrying them up to get some analysis that provides a clear insight into the assessment process. For example, a teacher collects data on students' test scores, lunch financial subsidy status, and absenteeism.

Once this data has been collected, the teacher organizes the data in such a way that allows them to find any links among the three data sets that may indicate certain patterns, and, in addition, the reasons why these patterns lead to any variance in student success rate. For example, after looking after evaluating those three pieces of data, you see that when free and reduced lunch students miss more than 5 days, their test scores drop 20%. By aggregating those three pieces of data to create a statistical analysis, we are able to tall a story and create interventions based on data. An example of an intervention may be putting students into tutoring once they miss three days of school while also trying to get to the root of their absences to try to stop them. This is the process of aggregation. It is about identifying any correlational relationships.

Therefore, what is important is not just to aggregate the data, but also to use it to identify the problem. Then, create suitable action plans. Next, put these actions in place to assist the students and ensure that their educational needs are being met. No student should be left behind, and this is a good way of ensuring that no one slips through the cracks.

Three Practical Steps to Success

1. Ensure that your faculty understands how to **map** the curriculum with **horizontal** and **vertical** alignment. To clarify, **curriculum mapping** is the process when you're making sure that what you're teaching is actually aligned to the **state** and **national** standards, and that your curriculum is also absolutely aligned.

Horizontal alignment is done within the grade level. So, this would be the process of discussing what is being taught and how by all teachers in the same grade level and seeing how it is affecting students differently within the grade level. Are students reaching the required level? If it becomes apparent that they have not reached the required level, then this is when you start thinking about ways to make this happen; for example, reteaching those topics to those students who may have not fully understood the first time. Next, you would also consider why they did not understand their instruction, perhaps factoring in ways of improving the methodology. Again, this can be sought from the horizontal alignment process.

Vertical alignment is a comparison between grade levels, so the process can go school-wide as a holistic institution. Further, you can actually compare school-to-school. But starting within the school level, you might assess what was being instructed in fourth grade, which indicates as to what needs to be taught in fifth grade. You are essentially looking for knowledge gaps and seeking any ways that you may need to modify some element to make sure the students are being taught appropriately at each grade level, even if something was missed that shouldn't have been. This way, you can map students' education from the moment they enter the school until the moment they leave.

2. Making sure faculty understands these terms and other terms and their associated concepts is key. Also, understanding how to actually carry out the processes is critical as well. Also, it is vital that teachers understand why these horizontal and vertical alignment processes are critical to delivering the best curriculum instruction and assessment.

For this last part, an educational leader may need to make these terms and their importance out-and-out explicit, and not take for granted that any of the terms or their associated concepts would be fully understood. It would be part of your role to show teachers exactly why they are required to know what these terms mean, and directly point out how to implement them.

This can be achieved under the premise that by reaching these aims, it will help the teachers to perform better in very practical ways. It is likely to bring in better results and student achievements.

As an educational leader, it is your duty to make sure that your faculty understands what is meant by the word "rigor." Rigor ensures your curriculum and instruction both match your state standards. **Form a committee to review your curriculum**

throughout the school year as well as from year to year. Your instructional practices should be monitored regularly to ensure rigor is taking place.

3. You should put in measures to **ensure that all teachers are using the appropriate technology whenever possible**. Offer professional development on technology, data, and assessments. Focus on getting those vital IT skills to your faculty to meet more students' needs.

We may assume that others have the expertise and know-how to collate and aggregate data. However, it is best never to assume anything, and to always look to provide learning opportunities surrounding data analysis and aggregation.

PSEL STANDARD 5

Standard 5 is about creating a **community of care and support for students**. Students are the core purpose of education, and without them, schools would be meaningless.

Students need looking after, no matter how old they are! Therefore, effective educational leaders must cultivate a school community that is inclusive and caring. The ultimate goal is to create an environment that promotes each student's academic success and well-being.

What processes and procedures must you have in place to ensure that students feel cared for and included?

Even if your whole school is doing innumerous things to make sure all the students feel cared for, this is pointless unless the students actually feel cared for. If the students don't feel the care, unfortunately, this is their **perception**, and that makes it your **reality**.

If this happens, you need to put things in place that alter the students' perceptions to change their reality. You also must consider what you are doing to ensure that students know and feel they are being cared for and included.

To start, you want to make sure that you are building and maintaining a safe and caring, healthy school environment. Check that all of your systems, including instructional and extracurricular systems, are open and allow your students to feel cared for, included, trusted, and respected.

You want to promote adult-student, student-peer, and school-community relationships. These three areas of interaction are extremely crucial! Setting up adequate relationships reinforces student engagement, which duly promotes positive student conduct.

At this stage, you may be thinking of your Positive Behavioral Interventions and Supports (PBIS) initiative. If you don't have a rigorous set already in place, you may want to consider including this program on your campus.

Below are some other kinds of processes you can put in place to help your school achieve Standard 5, which is about creating that adequate community of care and support for students.

Three Practical Steps to Success

1. Create a **student government**. Student governments often work well for schools because they not only get into the politics of it all, but they can make decisions and have input into issues that matter for students, from decisions within their grade level to the entire school.

2. Another thing you can consider is setting up a **student advocacy committee**, which differs from a student government. Student government operates more like a workers' union for the students, whereas a student advocacy committee focuses more on how the students are feeling. As you might imagine, this is an enormously advantageous way of gaining an insight into the students' perceptions.

There may be things highlighted to you that you may have not even realized were happening. The committee's purpose is to communicate these perceptions to the teachers. It is important for that student advocacy committee to gather together a normative group that can ensure all students on campus are represented.

3. Once you have these groups set up – student government and student advocacy committee – go about surveying your students about the school's climate and culture on a continuous basis. When you are getting that regular feedback, **create a plan to share results with adults** so that ideas can be generated on how to improve.

Remember that things can always be improved. Every school environment is dynamic and is set to evolve naturally, but here you have an opportunity to shape the climate and culture of the school so that students *feel* and *are* supported in a community of care that is created.

PSEL STANDARD 6

This standard is about developing the **professional capacity of school personnel**. This includes all the staff that works at the school, albeit you can primarily base it on the teachers and then apply it to other staff members.

Any effective educational leader must develop the capacity and professional practices of *all* school personnel to promote each student's academic success and well-being. A school is a complete institution with the purpose of delivering education to students, and so all staff – anyone who works in the school in any role – is involved in this.

Therefore, the primary question you should be asking yourself to achieve Standard 6 is: As a school leader, what are you doing on your campus to support and retain your teachers?

First, are you providing the correct support that allows your teachers to do their jobs properly? Second, are you doing enough so that the teachers gain and show professional pride and want to stay working at your school, rather than going off to try their hand working elsewhere?

Ultimately, staff retention is good for the students and good for the school as it provides consistency, so staff retention must remain a high priority for educational leaders.

Naturally, you may have a situation where as a leader, you need to dismiss people from their roles, and that would be because they are not performing to the required standard (or some other misconduct) and, therefore, not providing the level of education that they should.

This may be uncomfortable, but regardless, it also isn't good for consistency, albeit necessary in some situations – but not all. This is where the training, support, and capacity-building element come into play.

As an educational leader, you want to make sure you're doing all you can to support staff so that you're creating a good culture with productive staff, and you needn't get into a situation where staff is departing, either due to their own choice, or having that decision made for them.

Effective leaders are required to recruit, then support and develop, so that they can retain effective and caring teachers. A key factor in this is making sure that teachers and staff feel supported.

You can encourage staff to feel like they are in an environment where they are encouraged to continually learn and grow and feel enthusiastic about wanting to expand their knowledge and skillset by experimenting with new ideas and practices that might help them improve. You can do this in a way that takes out the fear of failure. Instead, teachers can be encouraged to develop and maintain a growth mindset.

This means the staff is operating in an environment where they know that they can make mistakes and are expected to make mistakes. They can make mistakes without fear of reprisal. Making mistakes is seen as a good thing; because if they're making mistakes, that means they're trying new things – which is exactly what you want to happen. Teachers are being proactive about improving their capacity, and this is exactly the kind of enthusiasm that should be encouraged and not shunned.

If there is any element in the culture that suggests that experimentation will be frowned upon or discouraged, this will ultimately lead to a reduction in the professional capacity of teachers, as well as potentially have a domino effect to the retention as staff starts to look to go elsewhere to satisfy their professional aspirations.

So, make sure you are creating the type of environment where your teachers can learn just as much as they teach; where staff can ask for help when it's needed; and where any idea is considered a good idea.

Give new ideas the light of day, and if someone has a suggestion, then try it out, because most times, you'll have nothing to lose, but more importantly, some of the best ideas on how to improve are generated by the practitioners.

Think of it as a bottom-up approach, rather than all the ideas need to come from the top. It then provides staff with some agency in the process too, and then the whole thinking process gains momentum. One idea leads to the next, which leads to the next, and so on.

In doing this, you'll be developing all the correct skills and professional knowledge that will help drive your school forward and create success. You'll also be creating the correct professional environment and developing the actionable feedback.

As well as creating professional opportunities, you also need to be promoting the health and well-being of your staff. This includes elements such as the work-life balance.

Leaders need to support staff in new ways more than ever. Phrases such as, "she's such a good teacher, she's always here at 5 am," are very cliché and, unfortunately, don't really add up. Just because the staff member is there at the crack of dawn, it doesn't necessarily equate to her being a skillful teacher. In fact, in some cases, showing that kind of presence, while being incredibly diligent, may actually mean the opposite – the question I'd be asking as a leader is why does that person feel the need to come in so early? Is this kind of additional attendance suggesting that the person is, in fact, struggling with any part of their work, or on the other hand, are they only showing up that early because they feel they need to, doing it for show?

Either way, this is where you step in as a leader, and behavior such as showing up early or staying late ought not to be commended (as in the "she's such a good teacher..." cliché), and also should not be ignored or have a blind eye turned to it either, as it could be a signal or "cry for help." If a member of staff is putting in those extra hours, then the first question on my mind would be *why* they are not able to complete their work within the usual hours, while other staff members are apparently managing their time better. As mentioned, it could come down to them either needing support, so that means you could be providing guidance on how they could improve work practices; or otherwise, it may just need a discussion to say, "It's ok, you don't need to be here all the time to impress me. In fact, I implore you to create a better work-life balance."

These days, creating a healthy work-life balance is actively encouraged in all industries, particularly people-facing roles, such as teaching. Just as much as everyone is expected to perform to a high standard, creating that downtime and having structured time off is considered just as important.

If anything, time away from work allows that worker to process and *recharge*, so they're ready for the next challenges they may face.

Several studies (generally speaking, I won't reference anything in particular here) have shown that staff who don't invest enough into their *downtime* demonstrate levels of stress and exhaustion that make them underperform. So, ultimately, getting enough rest and time away from work is actually more productive than constantly putting the hours in.

Here are three real-world examples that you can follow to achieve this standard, which is about developing the professional capacity of school personnel.

Three Practical Steps to Success

1. Starting with the first step, you can create a mentor-teacher, otherwise called a **Teacher Buddy System**.

This works incredibly well for new staff, as it gives them a point of reference and helps them build confidence quickly. Let the mentee know that their mentor is there for anything, any questions, any process issues, even just someone to vent to.

Make the mentor teacher active in the process and let them know what they need to do to support the new staff. Most teachers will have no problem taking on the role of the buddy as it is apparently something intrinsic that attracts people to become teachers in the first place to want to help others.

This buddy system needn't be only for new starts either, and you can apply buddies at any stage of a teacher's professional journey. The benefit of the buddy system is it may lead to some surprising results that you may never have realized.

For example, you might be surprised how many teachers are actually introverts, and that's why they never make their voices heard in more public arenas, such as team meetings. You may also learn when teachers are struggling with their work which you may never have realized had it not been for their "buddy" communicating with them and looking out for them.

Most times, the buddy system needn't be complicated, and it could be a case of pairing people up and having them ask each other a simple, "How are you doing today?" and then taking it from there. Give it a go in your school, and it could lead to all sorts of new discoveries and increased professional capacity of staff members.

2. Another idea to try is to **create a job-embedded professional development plan** with each teacher. This is something personalized for each staff member and something relatable to you as their manager. Not only are you setting goals in the development plan, but this is an opportunity for you to ask them, "What can I do to help you learn and grow?" Furthermore, you can ask them, "What do you want to learn?" and, more pertinently, "What do you *need* to learn?" These last two questions are paramount for the process to work, as it gives your staff agency and makes them involved in their own professional development.

It should never be a case of creating a professional growth plan and then bombarding teachers with a list of things they need to do. Doing things that way is a negative experience and doesn't create any enthusiasm for the change process. You want teachers to be on board. You want to be working with, not against, them.

Don't make the professional development plan simply a box-checking exercise to then be filed away and forgotten about until the next review. Instead, actually, make it a positive experience and ask the teacher their thoughts about how the professional development plan can be a *job-embedded* one.

3. **Create an observation and actionable feedback plan.** It is understandable that, just as teachers do, leaders also have a lot on their plate, but the crucial part of having any job-embedded professional development plan in place is to make sure there is an actionable part, and then that can come under review. Ensure that the feedback is also actionable; otherwise, the whole process lacks teeth and becomes meaningless.

Actionable feedback means, rather than just saying something is good or bad, telling them why and how they can do it better next time! Even if you think something was good, there's always room for improvement to make it even better each successive time.

There is no reason why giving and receiving actional feedback has to be a negative experience. The leader needs to ensure that they give feedback that contains something actionable; otherwise, it lacks substance. By doing this, alongside the other suggestions in your toolkit, you'll be well on the way to improving and developing the capacity of all staff at your school.

PSEL STANDARD 7

Standard 7 is about creating a **professional community** for teachers and staff.

Effective educational leaders foster a professional community of teachers and other professionals, which, in turn, promotes student academic success and well-being.

As a school leader, you'd need to have processes and procedures in place that create a growth mindset environment for the teachers.

Creating this growth mindset is really revolutionary for teaching, but is often overlooked, whereas it definitely should not be.

Very often, educational leaders don't give their teachers the time and the space to be innovative and to learn and grow. This is certainly something you should be seeking to do as an educational leader.

As a leader, make sure that your staff promotes effective professional development practices. This includes empowering and trusting students with leadership roles, which is a part of establishing a professional culture of engagement and commitment.

Again, this ties in with cultural responsiveness, so make sure that your teachers know what they're doing and, more importantly, why they're doing it. To ensure that teachers know the importance, make it actionable. Having this type of transparency is vital.

Achieving Standard 7 very much means including professional development for teachers, so that they can foster a community of professionalism.

Below are three real-world actions to further promote a culture of professionalism within your school.

Three Practical Steps to Success

1. Ensure that teachers have **time for collaboration with real purpose**. Don't make their collaboration purely reading each week, or only to sign in to prove a meeting took place. That achieves nothing, so make each meeting and collaboration opportunity really count for something. Make sure that teachers have a set time for collaboration, and second make sure that each time has an actual distinct purpose.

Ideally, some of that time is set aside just to be innovative. As part of this process, give tasks to teachers to bring to each meeting and then provide structured meetings to discuss the ideas.

This will give your meetings real rigor and will help to define the purpose. For example, one such task you could request of a teacher prior to the meeting is to come up with two ideas that could be tried out in the classroom to improve the learning takeaways.

2. Make sure that teachers understand **what kind of meeting** they're attending and **the purpose of the meeting**. This means that teachers know what to expect and know how to differentiate between meetings, such as a grade-level meeting, a content meeting, or any other kind of meeting. Just make sure the purpose is explicit – there should never be just a generic "meeting" without a defined purpose.

Along with making it extremely clear as to why each meeting is taking place, your teachers should also know why each individual was invited and, most of all, that each individual's opinion counts. Never get into a situation where you're just meeting for the sake of it, as that is a waste of time, pure and simple.

Ensure that every teacher has a leadership role at different times, according to different tasks at hand. This provides them a sense of purpose and is not intended to allow them to take over your job, but it's about making sure that every teacher has a leadership opportunity. Every staff member in a team deserves to be given an opportunity to shine through, and providing a leadership role is often the best way to bring out some of those best qualities.

Giving every teacher some type of leadership opportunity provides an opportunity for staff to learn what they're good at, where they have weaknesses that need to be improved, and how they can grow to know what they like and don't like doing. Essentially, this is about learning their leadership capabilities.

3. **Create a professional development committee**. If you do not want to fully set it up as a committee, you could set it up as a "think tank" as a space where ideas can be discussed and thoughts can flow freely. It is definitely worth setting up something like this, alongside any opportunity that allows your teachers to develop their leadership capabilities as well as generally creating a professional community at the school.

PSEL STANDARD 8

Standard 8 is centered on **meaningful engagement of families and community**. This is where your stakeholders start to enter into the fold.

Effective educational leaders engage families and the community in meaningful, reciprocal, and mutually beneficial ways which promote each student's academic success and well-being.

The major thing to be thinking about here as a school leader is how you can ensure that parents, business leaders, and your surrounding community all engage with your campus in meaningful ways.

The keyword here is meaningful – making that engagement count and show for something.

Effective leaders in this process must be approachable and accessible. They crave a sustainable, positive environment, and this makes a huge difference.

For example, you don't want that situation where you walk into your front office and nobody looks up; nobody says hello. You don't want that lack of engagement.

Even if you are in a conversation, you can always look up, say, "Hello, give me a minute, and I'll be right with you," to show you are fully aware and engaged, and you'd expect the same thing reciprocated.

The culture of the whole school is evident just from those front office engagements! This is down to the leadership style, as it is about how you would promote the culture of engagement within the school.

Always try to create an environment that promotes engagement in open, two-way communication.

Understanding, valuing, and employing the community's cultural, social, intellectual, and political resources are also crucial.

Three Practical Steps to Success

1. **Advocate** for the **needs of the school**, the **needs of the students**, and the **needs of the teachers**. As an educational leader, you need to be the voice for your school at the district, state, and national levels. Communicate with the community about their needs and your needs. Letting the community know that you are playing a part in the community is definitely crucial to creating that climate of meaningful engagement between families and the wider community.

2. Create a **calendar of community events** to participate in, so as to ensure that your community knows that you are involved with them. That way, this creates a kind of open invitation for them to get involved. It opens up that one-way street to become bi-directional. This is even more important if you don't live in the community where you are an educational leader because you want to make sure that your community knows that you are there for them.

They need to know that you're just not there for the relatively short time that you're at the school and with your students, and then you go home, and you're done. You need to send the message that you are there, part of the community, and always there for them. You want to make sure that the community understands that you are not just an educational leader, but you are a leader in the community.

3. Next, create a **list of resources available to your stakeholders**. You need to let them know what you have that might help your stakeholders or offer them further ways to engage with the school. For example, maybe you have some classes that are offered to parents, such as classes on how to navigate your website. Or perhaps your school offers community classes, and that needn't be limited to parents. It could be something that can engage anyone in the community, such as short IT courses.

PSEL STANDARD 9

Standard 9 is on the topic of **operations** and **management**. In many ways, this can be nicknamed the "silent standard" because most of us don't deal with operations and management until we become leaders. Somehow, even though we know that operations and management are a huge part of how the school is run on a daily basis, we manage to avoid it mostly until we become educational leaders. Then all of a sudden, it becomes very apparent. This important role need not be daunting, and there are several processes you can put into place to make the operations and management of your school more effective.

This standard is essentially focused on keeping your campus efficient. Effective educational leaders manage school operations and resources to promote each student's academic success and well-being. As a school leader, you must consider what practices, processes, and procedures you use to create an efficient independent learning environment.

For example, it could be anything from considering the flow of your campus during the bell schedule and lunch to hiring the right people for your culture. It could be something as tangible as looking at which doors lock and introducing the use of metal detectors to provide additional safety.

All of these things are not about the teaching or grading of the students, but have equal importance in the day-to-day running of the school, and as an educational leader, this would now fall on your shoulders.

Two of the things that you may wish to consider are to make sure that you are fiscally responsible and that you're using all of the resources available to you ethically and fairly. Also, you want to ensure that you're managing all of your staff resources, scheduling your teachers fairly, and abiding by other ethical considerations. Another responsibility would be to make sure you are protecting your staff members from any unnecessary disruption and doing your best to shield them from unwanted stress. One way to do this would be to employ the appropriate technology for communication and operations management and to ensure you are communicating effectively whenever possible. You want to implement a decent communication plan among people on your campus, but also among campuses.

Another crucial factor that fits in with this standard is knowing all of the applicable state and local laws so you never run the risk of breaking them. It is unlikely that you are going to know everything, but gaining as much knowledge as possible is extremely important, especially maintaining a link with someone in your district so that you can contact them to find out anything that you need to know.

You should also maintain a professional and productive relationship with your central office and your school board to understand the internal and external politics of your school as well.

Below are three real-world actions and examples you can put into place to help you meet the standard:

Three Practical Steps to Success

1. Develop a **reporting system for issues**. For example, let teachers know how they can report issues such as a broken window. Or allow teachers to identify some operational gaps, such as pandemonium in the hallway every lunch shift because there is no teacher on duty, or the teacher on duty is not standing in the correct place.

Creating a system to report problems will improve the operations of the school. Try not to rely on a simple system of in-person reporting when something happens, as that's when issues get lost and won't be dealt with effectively, creating frustration.

For example, the person could be too busy to report an issue immediately, or you could be the one who is too busy to accept the report. They might have to go somewhere immediately after, or they may try to find you and you're somewhere else, and then by the time there is an opportunity, all is forgotten. Or another example may be that they do tell you, but then you're so busy that you forget to act on it. Either way, the issue gets lost, which is exactly what you don't want to happen.

You certainly don't want this kind of state of affairs. You want a working system where nothing can "slip through the cracks." To avoid these kinds of scenarios, set up an adequate reporting system that ensures nothing ever gets missed, and likewise, every issue is actually acted on. One way to do this would be to use IT to set up the system, and then train everyone on the system so they know exactly how to use it and incidents can be reported in a timely and accurate manner.

2. **Develop adequate communication plans**. These shouldn't just be focused on telling staff how and when to attend the next meeting, but should go further than that. Rather than waiting for meetings, you could develop a system for communicating while ideas are still fresh and could be acted on much quicker than waiting for scheduled, in-person meetings.

You need to set up a system of relaying emergency information to teachers that is not public as well.

When developing the different communication plans, you also want to consider ways of getting information to staff when either you or they are off-campus. It definitely requires careful consideration of every eventuality when formulating the communication plans so there isn't an opportunity for anything to get missed.

3. **Develop and implement plans to handle building and personnel issues**. Create a committee focused on crisis plans, for situations where there is disagreement among staff. Verify that all staff know what to do in other crises or emergencies, such as all staff being aware of the protocol in the event of fire or fire drills and active shooters. These kinds of considerations are often overlooked, but they are fundamentally important to make sure the operations of your school do not break down.

Even if information such as what to do in a fire drill has been provided to staff, don't assume that telling them once will be enough. Always perform checks on your staff so that all know what to be doing in the eventuality that it happens.

PSEL STANDARD 10

The final standard is all about **school improvement**. Effective educational leaders act as agents of continuous improvement to promote each student's academic success and well-being.

The major question with this standard is how you stay current with research and maintain open dialogue with all stakeholders as a school leader. How do you afford yourself the opportunity to benefit from a variety of ideas?

Always seek to find ways to include the ideas of others, as there is no way you can do school improvement all by yourself. If you think that you don't need to value others' input, then that is your first mistake.

As a leader, you shouldn't be doing anything by yourself. You should always be open to considering other people's ideas. Remember that there are many stakeholders in the school, from students to teachers, and adults in the wider community.

What you need to consider and accept ideas on is how to make the school more effective for everyone. To do this, you can use different methods like those discussed in earlier standards, such as welcoming open communication with stakeholders and doing research for the improvement of your school.

You will also want to promote readiness, improvement, and the engagement of others because, as aforementioned, you cannot do this on your own – and don't be under the impression that you can.

As part of this process, you should be seek to have some type of school improvements committee that employs situation-appropriate strategies.

As an educational leader, you need to make sure that all involved are adopting systems that enable everyone to know what they need to do to improve.

Your role in this regard is to develop and promote leadership among the teachers and staff. To do this, you can take the suggestions from the three real-world actions below:

Three Practical Steps to Success

1. You should join and actively participate in **educational committee** meetings. You are the leader, so it is important that you know exactly what is going on. It would be impossible for you to know everything, but you should at least know what's going on with education in your state and on the national level.
2. Create a committee to **research current trends in education**. The purpose of this research committee is to find out new trends, gather data, and then consider how you can use it for your school's purposes to improve your practices.

3. **Set up a data committee** that reviews and monitors all data flowing into and out of the school. The data committee can oversee when student test scores are evaluated as well as climate surveys.

The purpose of these actions and committees are to identify room for improvement in the way that data is handled and delivered, as well as to provide insight into areas where targets can be met. Most targets are data-driven, so creating a committee for school-wide concerns is crucial. You will be able to clearly see the areas that you need to focus on for school improvement on your campus. The data could bring up all sorts of interesting revelations, including areas of focus for improving the school's culture, its climate, its security, and other areas, which at first glance, wouldn't be apparent.

PSEL SUMMARY

Throughout the course of this chapter, I have focused on the 10 PSEL and how to achieve them. Within each of these standards, there was a section called *"Three Practical Steps to Success,"* which provided real-world examples and suggestions of things you could put into place as an education leader to help you achieve the standard for your school.

Now, have a go at the thinking activity at the end of this chapter that marks the end of this section of the book. Doing each thinking activity that appears at the end of each part of the book will help to ensure that you've understood everything already discussed.

Also, if you need to go back and check anything from the previous chapter, now would be a really good time before you move on to the next part of the book, which is about the test itself.

Part One of this book was all about providing you with a suitable knowledge foundation about the PSEL, before delving more into the practical aspects of how to pass the test itself. So, it would be extremely advantageous that you understand everything in these past chapters before moving on to Part Two.

Once you have done the activity, you'll be in a good position to move on to Part Two.

THINKING ACTIVITY:

Go back through the ten PSEL and pick out some keywords and write them in a list.

Then, think about how these specific words link to each standard. Make a note of this next to the words you've selected.

You can view the "Successful School Leadership Through the PSEL Webinar" at www.educatoralexander.com/slla-test-prep.

PART II

LOGISTICS

3

REGISTERING AND PREPARING FOR THE TEST

*P*art Two of this book is all about the logistics of the SLLA Test and will provide further information about how to register for the test, how to prepare for the test day, and how to retrieve your test scores. This information can be updated at any time by ETS, so the website is provided to always gather the most updated information.

PREPARING FOR THE TEST EXPERIENCE

To prepare for the test, go to this website to see the videos about test day procedures and a computer test demo:  educatoralexander.com/slla-test-prep. This is important because it will prepare you for the actual test day, so no surprises will happen...you will feel comfortable with what to expect.

HOW TO REGISTER, RESCHEDULE, AND OTHER FEES

- Register at ets.org/sls/register
- The test costs $425.
- If you need to cancel, reschedule, or retake the exam, there are time restrictions and costs that may occur.
- There are testing accommodations available for test takers with disabilities, health-related needs, and whose primary language is not English.
- There is a schedule on the ETS website that shows exactly when your test scores will be released according to your test date.
- Find the most **current** information about registration, time restrictions, pricing, fees, scores, and more at the ETS SLS Test Registration website: ets.org/sls/register

EXAMPLES OF QUESTIONS

These types of questions are common to most computer-delivered PRAXIS tests, so they can be something you can expect.

TYPE 1: Standalone Questions

- The standalone question presents a *direct question* or an *incomplete statement*.

TYPE 2: Stimulus Materials

- Questions with stimulus materials begin with information such as a reading passage, graphic, table, or a combination of these, followed by a question based on that material.
- Sometimes two or more questions are based on the same stimulus material. In these cases, the stimulus will be on the left side of the screen, and the questions will appear on the right.
- Some questions require you to scroll down to view the entire stimulus and the following question.
- Make sure you scroll down to the bottom to be sure that you see *ALL* of the answer choices.

TYPE 3: Constructed Response

- Constructed response questions are questions that require you to provide a written response.
- For questions requiring a written response, the question being asked will appear on the top or left portion of the screen, and the area for you to type in a response appears on the lower half or right portion of the screen.

NEXT STEPS

In the next chapter, I'll be providing some details about how the tests are scored so that you can have this in your armory and know how best to pick up points when taking the test.

4
HOW TEST IS SCORED

Chapter Four is all about the logistics of the SLLA 6990 Test. In this chapter, you'll be given information about how the test is scored – something that many people find vital in order to pick up the maximum points.

At the end of this chapter, as it is the last chapter in this part of the book, there will be another thinking activity for you to try your hand. It is a good idea for you to pause at this stage and try the activity, as this will enhance your understanding of the test  before moving into the multiple choice and constructed response parts of this study guide.

HOW IS THE TEST SCORED?

As an educator with plenty of experience delivering training modules on the SLLA 6990, one of the questions I am asked the most is *how exactly is the test scored?*

This is a fair question, as knowing what the examiners are looking for is in many ways your key to success.

I get asked how many questions a person can miss yet still score enough to pass the test. For example, can a person get thirty multiple choice questions wrong yet still pass?

I asked ETS if there is a formula for passing the test. They said there is no way to tell how many questions one can miss because there are different versions to the test and they are all graded on different scales. So, how do you pass this test? By following the tips in this test prep book.

Here is the breakdown for the multiple choice part of the test, based on the standards you must meet, and the approximate number of the total 120 questions, with their percentile allocation worked out.

1. **Strategic Leadership – 20 questions (13%)**
2. **Instructional Leadership – 27 questions (17%)**
3. **Climate and Cultural Leadership – 22 questions (13%)**
4. **Ethical Leadership – 19 questions (12%)**
5. **Organizational Leadership – 16 questions (10%)**
6. **Community Engagement Leadership – 16 questions (10%)**

Unfortunately, there is no real way to tell if you'll pass the test or not based on the number of answers. Due to the method they use to score the tests, it is impossible to determine how many correct answers you'll need to obtain a certain score, and therefore pass the test.

My solution would be to not focus on this bare minimum approach; instead, aim to pass the test by taking each individual question as THE one to get you the passing score…focus on getting as many right as possible!

This may sound daunting but believe me, it isn't – I'm not kidding. You've already made the smart choice to buy this book as a study guide, and with all the tips presented in this book, I am confident that you'll be able to score top points on the test – if you study well.

TIMINGS OF THE TEST

There are two sections: The **multiple choice** section comes first (as mentioned above, 120 questions), and then you'll get a 10-minute break before being allowed to move on to the next section, which is **constructed response (4 questions)**.

You must take them in that order – **Section 1** followed by **Section 2**. You also have to stick to the times. That is to say, you cannot borrow time from Section 1 to use in Section 2. The ten minute break can also not be used for the test and can only be used to break.

To make this clear, for **Section 1,** you have **2 hours and 45 minutes**. As mentioned above, that is for **120 multiple choice questions**. That means you should spend around *1 minute per question*, using any remaining time to go through and check all your answers again – particularly checking the ones you weren't sure about.

For **Section 2,** you have **1 hour and 15 minutes**, which due to the number of questions, works out to be around *18 minutes per question*, using any remaining time to check through and add to your answers. So already, you can get an idea in your head about how much content they're expecting you to write for each of the four questions.

How much are you able to write in approximately 18 minutes? We're talking paragraphs, not pages.

Therefore, you do need to make sure you write enough for each constructed response to provide an adequate answer to gain those valuable points, and this needs to be done all within the 1 hour and 15 minutes.

You now know the times you will be given for the 6990, so you can keep this in mind when doing your practice tests. You can time yourself and see how long it's taking you to complete each section and at which parts you need to improve.

So, **the total time for the test is 4 hours**. Make sure you're able to complete the entire test within those 4 hours. More so, remember how that time is divided – with **2 hours 45 minutes for the first section** and **1 hour 15 minutes for the second section**.

SCORE RANGES AND STRUCTURES

Your possible score range is 100 through 200. Your test report will indicate PASSED or NOT PASSED by comparing your score to the passing score used by the state in which you currently live. Each state that requires an SLS test sets its own passing score. To obtain the most recent information that ETS has regarding the passing score required by each of the participating states, you can check its website (www.ets.org/sls)

The constructed response part of the test is rated/scored independently by two scorers. If the two ratings disagree by more than one point, your response is then rated by a third scorer, whose rating is then used to resolve the discrepancy.

Scores are available for reporting for ten years, although do note that some states require that test scores be earned within a specified time – so do check the requirements in your state.

Also, you can designate who to send your test scores to when you register for the test. So you can send scores to your state department of education, to any educational leadership program you are a part of or anyone else.

THE QUESTION WEIGHTINGS

For Section Two – the **Constructed Response** – there are four questions that fall into four standards.

(A) Strategic Leadership
(B) Instructional Leadership
(C) Climate and Culture Leadership
(D) Ethical Leadership

You'll see these four standards addressed in much greater detail in Part Four of this book, but for now, I'll address all **six standards** that you must meet in Section One.

As already listed above, the multiple choice section will ask you about all of the following standards: (I) Strategic Leadership, (II) Instructional Leadership, (III) Climate and

Cultural Leadership, (IV) Ethical Leadership, (V) Organizational Leadership, and (VI) Community Engagement Leadership.

HOW THE MULTIPLE CHOICE WILL APPEAR

Even though all of the multiple choice (sometimes referred to as *selected-response*) are the same in structure, in that you are posed with a question but also presented with answers to choose from, there are actually two different types of questions.

The first type of multiple choice question asks you to drag and drop your answers into the correct order. An example of that type of question includes:

"How do you implement… e.g., *a program?*"

So, you'd then be required to put the steps in the right order by dragging the answers and dropping them into the boxes. You can think of this type of question like a constructed response question where they ask you a scenario, but actually give you the correct answers/steps. Your task is to put them in order of importance or in sequence of action.

We'll look at some examples of these types of questions in the next part of this book, which is dedicated to the multiple choice part of the test.

The second type of multiple choice question asks you a question and then gives you a choice of answers and you select the right one. Or in some cases it may ask you to select multiple answers (e.g., "select three of the following" / "select all that apply").

HOW THE CONSTRUCTED RESPONSE WILL APPEAR

There are two kinds of constructed response formats: *with* or *without* documents. First, I'll explain how it may look and what to do with a ***document-based constructed response question***.

Your screen will display documents. For example, it may show you documents one, two, and three – all in tabs.

The kind of documents you might expect to see include test scores, a parent letter, or an observation from the principal.

Also, notice your scenarios here, too. The information will tell you things such as which school you're at and what's going on. It will set the scene.

The question is then presented alongside the document, and there is a small box where you can type your answer.

As mentioned above, you have approximately 18 minutes to type in each of your constructed responses. It is a relatively small space to read everything needed and type your answer, so get used to the typing skill that will be required.

Prepare yourself for how you're going to type into the box – both mentally and also with technique. As well as regular typing, you can only cut, paste, undo, and redo as commands.

If your constructed response question **doesn't have any documents to refer to**, it will appear as a simple, straightforward scenario question that you need to answer. When it appears this way, you'll have a bigger space to type your response into.

FURTHER POINTERS

Below are some additional guidelines to take into account to best prepare you for what to expect from the test.

A Perfect World Mindset

One of the biggest factors for understanding the questions and passing this test is getting into right mindsets. One of those mindsets is the *perfect world mindset*.

In a perfect world, time is not that big of an issue. Poverty is not that big of an issue. Consider how you would answer these questions if you have all the time and money in the world. All of the issues we deal with in the real world are not on this test. You must put on rose-colored glasses to answer these questions.

For example, if Johnny took the test and Johnny failed, it is because Ms. Smith did not teach a rigorous curriculum. It is not because Johnny may not have eaten that day, so he may not have been able to concentrate because he was too hungry. Nor would it be because Johnny was too tired to concentrate and didn't have time to study because he has a job since he's trying to support his mom and his daughter.

Those things may be the reality, but none of that exists on this test, where they assume a perfect world.

It is a very black and white world on the test, which may not be an exact reflection of how things would play out in the real world, but it's not the real world for the 6990 test; it is an imaginary, perfect world. So, it is worth bearing this in mind as you formulate your answers.

The Leader's Mindset

Bear in mind that this test is already being delivered in half of the United States. The test doesn't want to know things about your particular school or district. So if you begin saying, "At my school, we do it this way," you are already making a mistake.

It is a generic test that covers multiple different things, so keep your answers broad. They don't want to hear about your particular school or district.

I usually say that 60% of this test comes down to mindset. Mostly, to pass the test, it is all about getting in the right frame of mind. If you're in the correct mindset, then you're in the best place to answer.

Another mindset you need to get into is the *administrator mindset*. You're no longer thinking about just your students, or only your subject or your grade level, or even just your school. You're thinking about things with a more global mindset. As a leader, you must think about every decision as being a global decision. It is no longer just for one or two students. So, even if it is one or two students initially, whatever decision you make is still going to have a wider, global effect.

You have to think about how this one decision that you're making, no matter how small or insignificant it seems, is going to have a domino effect to impact everybody. With every decision that you make, you have to consider how it's going to affect your students, teachers, staff, and parents – or any other stakeholders.

SUMMARY

As I've already mentioned, a huge part of passing this test is getting into the right mindset.

First, you want to be in the *perfect world mindset,* as described above – forget any real-world factors, as that isn't what the examiners are considering.

Second, you want to be in the *leader mindset*. You don't want to be in the mindset of just thinking about your campus or your district or your school.

Overall, it is crucial that you get in the right headspace when taking the test, as this will ensure that you are producing the right kind of answers.

Before you even attempt to answer the questions, be aware of the kinds of answers that the examiners are looking for – adapt your mentality – and this will give you a much higher chance of scoring points.

This brings us to the close of the logistics section of this book. So far, we've traveled through two chapters that describe everything from what to expect on the day of your test, how to register and retrieve scores, as well as looking at how the test is scored all throughout this chapter.

Before you move on to unlock the secrets of just how you can be sure to score maximum points, spend some time to pause and reflect, and complete the thinking activity below.

THINKING ACTIVITY:

Review the logistics of the test and create a test-taking plan for yourself. How will you test, when will you test, what will you wear and so forth?

Consider the two mindsets you need to be in when you take the test. Think of two real-world situations where you would be a leader. How would you respond to these two situations from a leadership mindset and a perfect world mindset?

PART III

MULTIPLE CHOICE

5

TIPS ON PASSING THE MULTIPLE CHOICE SECTION

*Y*ou've now come this far and are ready to dive into the content of the SLLA 6990 Test.

As a reminder, the **multiple choice section** of the test will be comprised of 120 **questions**.

EMPHASIS ON SHARED VISION AND INSTRUCTION

A great entry point to understanding the multiple choice section of the test is to learn some tips and then take it from there.

My first tip is that there is a strong emphasis on shared vision in teaching. Because as an educational leader, one of the biggest things that you're going to deal with is instruction.

The entire purpose of education is to deliver instruction for gaining student achievement. Even though how we define instruction and student achievement vary, it is a large part of being an educational leader and, consequently, there is a large emphasis on it on the test. Now, you cannot have an impact on instruction if educators do not understand the vision of the school and of the decision-making. Therefore, there is also a large emphasis on shared vision. If we do not know why we're doing what we're doing or know where we are trying to go (the goal we are trying to reach), then we have no clue why we are doing what we are doing?

This is why the emphasis is on shared vision, based on the fundamental factors of instruction and teaching for the purpose of student achievement.

PILOT QUESTIONS

The multiple choice section may contain approximately ten pilot questions included in the test. You're not going to know which ones they are. These pilot questions are ones ETS is trying to test out to see if they are good questions or ones not to include in later tests.

These questions will not count against you. You won't know which ones they are, and you won't know if your test has them or not. Nevertheless, it is good to know that you may get a question that really throws you. If you see something like that, perhaps it doesn't make sense, then don't worry too much as it may be a pilot question – something they're trying out but won't count.

START AT A RANDOM POINT

Most often, we like to do things in a linear fashion. That would mean starting at question 1 and ending with the last question.

However, you could try starting at a random question in the middle. This may help you focus better as you're not concentrating on the time per question too much. It will be harder to tell how far you've progressed through the test based on the question number alone. This is just a trick you can use if you wish to help you get out of your head a little by not focusing too much on the time per question, but concentrating on the content of the questions themselves.

CHOOSE ACTIVE ANSWERS VERSUS PASSIVE ANSWERS

On those questions where you're having a problem choosing between two answers, the tip is to choose the active answer.

For most questions, you will be presented with four possible answers, but if you get to a point where you're choosing between two of them but not sure which one, look for the active answer rather than the passive one.

As an example, if you were asked, *"What is the best way to get the word out about an open house,"* and your four possible answers are **(A) put out a newsletter, (B) do a call out to all parents using an electronic system, (C) visit each student's parents' house to let them know about the open house, and (D) send a letter home**, the most active answer here would be C, so that would be the one to go for.

Remember, as mentioned in the previous chapter, this test assumes a perfect-world scenario. Of course, there may be many barriers to you visiting each student's parents' house. It may not be realistic, but in a perfect world, that is what you'd do. It is the most *active answer* in a *perfect world*, and so **C** is the correct answer here.

In an ideal world, as mentioned in the logistics part of this book, going to each student's parents' house is the best option, because not only do you see where your students live, and you get more of an insight into their home life, but you're actually seeing parents face-to-face and having that communication while achieving your main objective of letting them know about the open house.

The only drawback to this tip is the answer also has to be THE RIGHT ANSWER and ANSWER THE QUESTION. Don't just look for active answers and choose them. This is test is not to be skimmed or reduced to looking for key words. You must read very, very carefully as one word can make the answer incorrect.

STUDY THE REASONING

When you're looking at practice questions, especially if you're looking at them from the ETS study guide, flip to the back of the book and study the actual *reasoning* behind the answers, versus studying the questions per se.

You're not going to see those same questions again, but you will see the reasoning behind that question, and this will help you understand and pass similar questions next time.

The reasoning behind the question is directly related to what they want to make sure that you know (the PSELs). So, you're going to see the reasoning (or something similar to it) in a whole new scenario question on the real test.

Study the reason behind a question, and this will give you greater understanding of other, similar questions you may be asked.

TAKE NOTE OF THE VOCABULARY

If you have time left over at the end of your multiple choice section, write down the vocabulary that is used and then reapply it to your own answers in the constructed response part of the test.

One of my test takers gave me this really clever idea as it means you're using the same language, the verbiage, that the examiners are looking for. Therefore, it may help you pick up some points in the constructed response section of the test.

GROUP BY SKILL LEVEL

This is getting a little bit more into the particular content of the test, but if you think about grouping or assigning teachers to projects, then group them by the skill level of the teacher to the task at hand.

This means whatever situation, whatever task you have, you're going to be able to find the teacher to assign according to their skill level. The question may not specifically tell you to group teachers or assign teachers, but when you read the question and the answer choices, you'll be able to break it down to recognize that it is about how you assign a teacher to a task.

For example, if you're arranging a science fair, you're going to get the science teacher, not the teacher who has the most degrees. If you're doing a bake sale, then you're going to get the family and consumer science teacher, not the teacher who has been there the longest.

This may sound obvious, but just be clear about your groupings and why you're doing it that way. The science teacher may have the most degrees, and the family and consumer science teacher may have been there the longest, but that isn't your primary reason for appointing them.

There is no need to assign your teachers to tasks arbitrarily; you can assign them by the skill that matches the task in hand.

NEXT STEPS

These tips featured in this chapter are just my initial tips for picking up points in the multiple choice section. As you go through the rest of the chapters, you'll see some more in-depth tips based on particular topics.

6
RESOLVING CONFLICTS

*I*n the previous chapter, you were introduced to the multiple choice section that appears on the test by going through some general hints and tips. Now, in this chapter and those that follow, I'll go more deeply into the content that you may expect to encounter in the multiple choice questions and those educational leaders should know.

I'll start with **conflict** and **resolution**. Naturally, working in a people-centered industry such as the education field, you are bound to be presented with conflict.

Conflict is to be expected, yet it is how you manage the conflict that is the all-important factor. As you would imagine, your ability to resolve conflicts effectively is one of the things the examiners are looking to assess on the SLLA 6990. Therefore, it is a good idea to get into the mindset that when it comes to conflict, it should not be viewed as a negative word.

CONFLICT IS NOT A BAD WORD

Conflict is not a bad word and conflict is not negative. It brings about change that can be a positive thing. So, as an educational leader, when you see conflict on the test, you do not intervene. You monitor and only intervene when necessary. You do not want the conflict to become personal or negative, so you will monitor it. But only intervene when necessary. Give the people in the conflict time to work it out themselves and see what solution comes from it.

DON'T FORGET YOUR PURPOSE

Sometimes we get so caught up in our roles, particularly when we move on from a classroom teacher role into an educational leadership role, we forget our true purpose.

Always remember your purpose as an educator – no matter what your role – as this should be the framework from which everything else operates. Also, keep this framework in mind when it comes to taking your SLLA test.

The whole purpose of anyone working in the education field is educational instruction and student achievement. That's why we're all here.

Questioning what is success, what is achievement, how does it look per student, how does it look as a class and as a school, and how do we get our students there will help  educational leaders have a student-centered focus to guide all of the decisions that are made.

Education would lack purpose if it weren't for ensuring that students achieve, and this comes from the instruction they are given. Keep this fundamental principle in your head as you go about answering the test questions.

WALKTHROUGH QUESTIONS

The purpose of a walkthrough is to open a dialogue with a teacher about instruction. It is not about making yourself seem more visible or relevant, nor is it about seeking out any maintenance issues. Likewise, it is not about foreseeing behavior issues in students.

What it is about is the *instruction* – and ensuring you can start discussing the positives and negatives of a teacher's instruction to aid them in their instructional practice.

Opening up the dialogue with a teacher ought to be a positive process. You can start by pointing out all the things they do well before mentioning anything they could improve on that would need to change.

DUE PROCESS

Sometimes you need to talk to a teacher because of their bad behavior. Either you've seen it yourself, or someone has reported the bad behavior to you, or someone has actually complained about the teacher.

In any case, you must give that teacher (or it may be another member of staff) due process. This means you have to talk to them first; you must make them aware of what the complaint against them is.

If you are thinking you should investigate the complaint first, as perhaps you don't want to bother faculty or staff unnecessarily, or you're seeking some truth behind the claims and doing all of this before you actually approach the teacher to mention the situation, this is wrong.

You would give the teacher due process and approach them first. It does make sense to go to the teacher to discuss any issue of contention first before mentioning it to anyone else or before conducting your own investigation without their prior involvement for many practical reasons.

For example, what if there was a complaint about a teacher, and while you were investigating, trying to get to the bottom of the claims, someone went straight to the teacher to tell them about it? Can you imagine how the teacher would feel? Actually, somewhat ironically, this could even lead to more conflict, which is exactly the opposite of what you're trying to achieve.

What if a parent complains about a teacher and you did not tell that teacher, but the students knew? Hopefully you can imagine the kind of further conflict this might lead to during the students' next interaction with the teacher.

Always go straight to the teacher first and give them due process. Approach the teacher and tell them that there was a complaint against them, or in another case, you could go to them directly and tell them about something you observed them doing that is not correct.

The only time on the test that due process does not come into play is if you see something that is illegal. Some examples of this may be seeing your teachers drinking or doing drugs on campus (even if it was at an after-hours social event, such as the school dance). In the case of illegal activity or something that will cause immediate harm (physically hurting a student, for example), you can immediately follow district protocol, such as calling the authorities.

However, you are not likely to get too many questions like these situations on the test. The questions you are likely to get will mostly be asking you to resolve different kinds of conflict, and they'll be looking for you to enact the due process as the first step.

CONFLICT BETWEEN GROUPS

You may get scenario questions where you have multiple teachers or multiple groups going against each other.

This may be, for example, a parent group and a teacher group going against each other, or it might say something like, "you are a first-year principal and you make a decision, and then a group of teachers speak out against your decision," or "a group of teachers don't follow your decision."

The solution here is to always talk to people or groups individually, and then you can bring them together later. First, what you should do is talk to them separately to hear each of their independent views on the matter, and then after that, you could bring them back together as a group. For example, you would speak to the parent group and then speak to the teacher group, then bring them back together to speak to them as a collective group. If it is individuals, then you would talk to the individuals separately, then together.

Keep this technique in mind when you get those questions about conflicts between groups.

OUT-OF-CONTROL CLASSROOMS

You may get a question about a teacher who has been assigned a mentor, and the teacher's classroom is still repeatedly out of control. The question may ask what you should tell the mentor to do.

You should tell the mentor to tell the teacher to speak with you, the educational leader. You are the instructional leader, the discipline leader, and any other type of leader your school needs. So, if the mentor's help is not being successful in this area, you need to help as well.

Also, if a question would ask you what to focus on first (instruction, lesson plan development, classroom management), of course the answer will be classroom management as it deals directly with behavior. Now, for some reason, on standardized tests, we talk ourselves out of the right answer. Of course if the instruction would improve, the behavior may improve, but instruction is not the first focus...classroom management of the behavior is.

FIND THE KEY WORDS

On this test, you must read carefully! This is not a test you can simply skim and only look for key words. Skipping one word in the question or in the answer choices can make it wrong.

So, when we talk about key words, we mean words in the question that can change the entire meaning of the question itself, like "first," "initial," and "except."

If you see "first" or "initial" in your questions, most of your answer choices will be correct. Sounds weird, right? But because the question did not ask you to choose the CORRECT answer, that means you will be given multiple answer choices that are correct. The question asked you which would you do FIRST or what your INITIAL step would be (not for the correct step). That means while many of the answers can be correct, you are looking for the one action you would take FIRST.

To help with these types of questions, close your eyes and imagine you are standing in the front office. Someone comes up to you and whispers the scenario in your ear. When you open your eyes and take that first step, which answer are you going to do. That is your correct answer.

Now, if your question has the word "except" in it, this means you are looking for the wrong answer. The question is asking you which of these would you NOT do--which one is the exception. That means, for this type of question, the correct answer is the wrong action. This can be a little tricky for some. This is another question where you will have multiple correct answers because they are asking you to pick the wrong one, so there will only be one that is wrong.

Let's look at this quick example.

You are in the middle of state standardized testing. You have room monitors and hallway proctors who have all been certified to give the exam. It is reported to you that Ms. Smith, a room monitor, is helping her students cheat on the exam. What is your initial step?

a) call the superintendent and make her aware of the situation
b) pick up all of the students' tests in that classroom and start an investigation
c) take Ms. Smith out of the class and put in a hall monitor while you start the investigation
d) contact your test administrator to start the process

The answer here is C, because it indicates that you're going to remove the problem first. While all of the other steps would possibly be taken, you must remove the problem from the situation first. Also, while doing that, you can give Ms. Smith due process and start the investigation by contacting your test administrator and calling the superintendent which could possibly lead to the test being picked up. You see how all of these are good steps, but the question asked what would you do FIRST!

Think about it from another perspective, and if you chose another option first, like A. If you were to do that and you called the superintendent, wouldn't you think her first question might be, "Where is Ms. Smith right now?" If your answer is she is still in the classroom (possibly about to start a new test that will be voided), the superintendent would ask you why in the world she is still in the room with testing students.

You may need to follow up with some of the other actions afterward, but the first step would always be to do something that prevents any further potential instances of misconduct, and this also provides the opportunity to give the teacher due process.

Finding the keywords in the question can help you understand what the question is actually asking you and can lead to you finding the correct answer.

SUMMARY: MANAGING CONFLICT AND REACHING RESOLUTION

We've now reached the end of this chapter which has been about tackling those questions on the test that want to know how you'd go about resolving conflict.

As a reminder, *conflict* shouldn't be seen as a bad word, only that it presents a challenge you can overcome. Otherwise, a certain amount of conflict is healthy as it brings about change, which is always needed. So, conflict should be considered a natural, positive necessity.

Keep in mind everyone's *purpose* in education is to ***provide instruction*** for ***student achievement***. So keep that in mind while answering questions. Also remember to look for the keywords in the question as it can drastically change the meaning of the question itself.

The next chapter is another theme that will appear in the multiple choice questions of the test: observations and feedback. Before moving on, please make sure you have fully understood the information in this chapter regarding conflict and resolution.

7
OBSERVATIONS AND FEEDBACK

*I*n this chapter, we will look into how you can best answer questions about observations and feedback.

At the end of this part of the book, there are some "thinking activities" for you to try your hand at, and this will help you with your general understanding.

It is also recommended that you understand all the key terms and phrases from each chapter. All of the vocabulary terms are defined within the context of the chapter.

THE PURPOSE OF PRE- AND POST-OBSERVATIONS

In the last chapter, we considered what the entire purpose of education is–*instruction* and **student achievement**–and the purpose of doing observations fits in with this.

The purpose of a *pre*-observation meeting is to discuss the lesson plan with the teacher. The leader needs to find out what should the observer see when they are in the classroom. The pre-observation meeting is to find out what should the teacher be doing, what should the students be doing, and what outcomes should be obtained.

The purpose of a *post*-observation meeting is to **reflect on instruction**. So, it would contain information such as what was observed versus what the expectation was. Then, it is an opportunity for feedback about what worked well, what needs improvement, and offering suggestions for the improvement.

PLNS

A PLN is either a *personal* or *professional learning network*. A PLN could either be people at your campus, other people in your physical network, or people online. In some way or another, your PLN will be about your educational collaboration.

This means that a PLN gives you an indication about who you will go to when it comes to learning, or who you might approach to bounce ideas off. So, if you have a group of teachers at your school, you could go to them to develop ideas.

Feedback can go both ways, as you can either offer them advice, or you may get tips from them. It is a mutual process.

Also, your PLN could be online, using social media platforms like Twitter or Facebook. No matter what way you're constructing your PLN, it will still meet the purpose, which is educational collaboration.

STRATEGIC PLAN

A strategic plan is what a district uses to lay out its goals, vision, mission and agendas for a specific amount of time. Most schools have school-improvement plans that do the same thing on the campus level.

To support your district's strategic plan as an educational leader, you are going to follow what it says to focus on for improvement. For example, if a goal in the district strategic plan is to raise reading scores, then that will be a focus of your department or your school campus.

SHOWING SENSITIVITY TO THE EXPRESSED NEEDS OF OTHERS

As an educational leader, you will have many of your stakeholders expressing their wants and needs to you. One of your jobs is to show them that you are sensitive to what they tell you.

Here are three steps to show that you are sensitive to the expressed needs of others:

- **Actively listen**. Make sure you're giving full and undivided attention to the person, and you are actively listening to them.
- **Act**. Find out how best you can support the person with their concern and take action.
- **Provide feedback**. Whether that feedback is positive or negative, in order to support the person, you need to let them know that you've looked into it, and here are the results.

Even if this means that the person is upset with you about the result, they will still know that you not only actively listened to them, but that you took action on what they requested, and then you are responding back to them.

The feedback step is an important part of the process as it proves that you respect the person enough to respond to their expressed need. It may not have been the feedback they were hoping for, but it provides legitimacy and shows you are interested in putting them and their needs first.

EFFECTIVE LEADERSHIP

Let's take a look at a quick sample question, such as, "Can an effective leader make a decision, hear new information, and then change his or her mind?"

The answer to that is "yes."

We want a leader that is responsive. If they hear new information, then they are willing to and will actually change their mind if and when needed. They will change their mind based on the new information and is responsive to the situation in hand.

This is what makes an effective leader; that is to say that a leader is able to gather new information/new data and understand that it shows a previous decision is not working. More than that, an effective leader is then able to alter their decision for the betterment of all involved.

PUTTING IT ALL TOGETHER: OBSERVATIONS AND FEEDBACK

When they ask the multiple choice questions, please make sure that you are following the directions. They may format the questions in a way such as, "tell us which three of the following, or which two of the following…," and so on.

Be sure to read the directions carefully, as you would not want to fail one of the multiple choice questions simply because you had not followed the directions properly.

Each question is likely to be slightly different from the instructional information, so it is important not to gloss over this point.

When it comes to any questions that you may be asked about classroom observations, the thing that I really like about this test is that they are asking you to be more hands-on. So, this is a great indicator of how you need to go about providing the correct answer.

What they are likely to do is actually give you a classroom observation that a principal or school leader has completed, and then ask you to have a look in and see what you should be observing in that lesson.

As you might expect, the things you are going to be looking out for are "openers" or "bell-ringers," anything that makes the lesson more interactive, things that make the lesson more student-led, and some type of effectual closing to the lesson.

Also, if they have any type of assessment within the lesson, you want to make sure that it actually matches the goal or the objective of the lesson.

Therefore, you want to put on your leadership hat when it comes to these questions, and here are a couple of things that you should always be looking for:

- **What should be in that lesson, and does it all make sense**?
- **How are you going to give feedback?** They may give you a classroom observation and ask you what kind of feedback you would give to the teacher.

When it comes to feedback, you need to make sure that the lesson and assessment match up to the objectives.

For example, if the objective of a math lesson was to learn addition, but when you went into the classroom to observe, you saw that students were using subtraction, then this is definitely one of the things that you would need to address with the teacher.

The feedback is their goal and objective for the lesson did not match the lesson you observed. The discussion would be to find out why.

As another example, if the lesson that you observed came off more like a lecture, then you need to address with them why it was not more student-led.

Overall, the classroom observations and feedback are based on matching what should be in the lesson as to what actually occurred.

Do not think that just because you're looking at it from a leader standpoint that you're looking for anything different than you would if you were a teacher and peer.

As a teacher, you'd know what a good lesson is, and you can just adapt that into your leadership role.

8

FORMULATING AND MONITORING LONG-TERM GOALS

The last chapter was on observations and feedback. Now, in this chapter, we're going to focus on the topic of formulating and monitoring long-term goals.

MAKING AND ASSESSING LONG-TERM GOALS

The big question here is how do you make and assess long-term goals? In order to achieve this, use SMART goals.

SMART stands for **Specific**, **Measurable**, **Achievable** (and action-oriented), **Realistic**, and **Timely.** We will discuss SMART goals a bit more later. While you are making sure that your long-term goals are SMART, you also must make sure they match your vision and mission. The vision and mission should guide every decision and goal made (which is why they are so important).

And to assess any goal, especially long-term ones, you must use student data. Every decision we make is ultimately for the benefit of our students, so student data will tell us if any of our decisions have been effective.

These three (SMART goals, matching your goal with your vision and mission and assessing with student data) will help in answering questions like is a program effective, is the new curriculum working and are we hitting our long-term goals.

LEADERSHIP VS. MANAGEMENT

A leader and a manager are two different things. A leader can always manage a situation if need be, but a manager cannot always lead. To lead is to inspire and to manage is to control. This is really critical to know when answering the multiple choice questions.

If one of the answers says that you "manage" something, then that is probably not the answer, because you need to make sure that the answer fits with the question all the time. Therefore, if you see that the leader is going to *manage*, that is a big red flag for that answer. It is probably not the right answer.

CULTURE

Being a leader has a lot to do with data and culture and you will see this reflected on the test. So you will see various questions about improving the culture of your school, being inclusive and improving instruction using data. We will discuss all of these more in-depth during this part of the book.

DIVERSITY

Coded language is when common words and phrases are used to mean something else, usually negative. Well, there is a phrase in education that usually means more diverse students are entering the school population and the negative or positive intent of the phrase depends on those speaking it. You will see this phrase on the test too.

If you see the phrase "the demographics are changing" or "the demographics have changed," it means that students of different races, religions, genders, sexual orientations, and more that makes up a person culture have a larger population in the school now.

The good thing about this test is that it is very current with addressing issues with "demographic changes" in schools that happen in real life, such as cultural responsiveness and equity. We will discuss this more in-depth.

INFORMING THE COMMUNITY OF YOUR GOALS

Let's take an example of how you'd be providing information to the public without using technology. The school marquee can be used in this way. It is that sign that you have in front of your school, whether electronic or regular signage.

It is one of the mediums that can be used to provide information about your school, even your school vision. If you want to get your school vision out to the public, a school marquee is a great way to do that, or another method might be displaying banners.

Think about who may see the banner or school marquee and therefore get an opportunity to learn your school vision. If they are not a parent, not part of the immediate community, then they are not going to be receiving other information, but remember that a school is a part of everyone's community.

PRACTICAL ANSWERS

Another thing you'll find with this test that I rather like is that it has more of a practical focus than the previous versions. It tests you on more realistic situations that you will find in schools today. Now, this test was created pre-pandemic so you will not find many or any questions dealing with post-pandemic situations until it updates again.

Some questions on the test do not simply ask you WHAT the answer is. However, they will give you the answer and then ask you why that answer is important or why the leader chose that particular action.

For example, they may give you a scenario and tell you what the leader did to solve the issue. Then, the question may ask you why they did it this way. Or another thing they may ask is why it is important for them to do it this way, or why they would choose to do this.

Make sure that you read each question carefully because one or two words can completely change the question. For example, the question might ask, "How do you make your classroom culturally responsive?"

I would answer that one way. However, if asked, "How do I make my teachers more culturally responsive in their instruction," I would answer that in a completely different way.

The question on how to make your classroom more culturally responsive could be that I check my own biases. On the question of how to make your teachers more culturally responsive in their instruction, we can discuss cultural responsiveness in general by making sure that lessons match students' interests and that students have a choice in what they're learning. We will discuss both of these topics more later.

Now that we have reviewed more tip based content in the last few chapters, let's take a deeper dive into content you are likely to see on the test and content that every educational leader should know and consider.

9

SMART GOALS

HOW TO MAKE A SMART GOAL

*I*n the last chapter, we looked at making and assessing long-term goals, which followed on from doing observations and providing feedback, and now we're going to take a deeper dive into understanding SMART goals.

In questions about goals, you may not see the G-word (goals) being mentioned; they may not make it that obvious to you. Even though they may not use the word "goal," if they are asking you about which one of the multiple choice answers is the best plan for this campus to

take, you want to pick a goal that's a SMART goal (specific, measurable, action-oriented, realistic, and timely).

Let's look at the SMART goals in action to answer a question. So, if I have these answers: A) better student graduation rates B) good citizenship. No matter what the question is, which is the SMART goal?

Better student graduation rate seems like a good goal for every school. However, as I have told you, when it comes to the SLLA 6990, we are in a perfect world. Therefore, surely, we all want good citizens.

If we are talking about a test in a perfect world, good citizens make much more sense to me. Right? However, better student graduation rates are indeed the answer here because it is the only SMART goal. Don't talk yourself out of the right answer.

Even in a perfect world, your goal must be a SMART goal. You can't measure what a good citizen is; therefore, it is not SMART.

The principle of what constitutes a good citizen is debatable. You may think a good citizen is someone who has graduated from college, but someone else may perceive a good citizen as someone who donates to the needy. Or, you may think a good citizen is someone who's never been to jail, but I may say I don't care if they go to jail if they take care of their family and community.

So, you can see here the difficulty with measuring this, and it doesn't fit in with the SMART goals.

However, achieving better student graduation rates is a SMART goal. Graduation rates are specific. The number of how many students graduated is measurable. It is action-oriented as the action is graduation. It is also realistic and also timely. We know exactly when graduation is, and it is realistic because we, as educators, can do our part to achieve this. Otherwise, we wouldn't be here.

As you can see, if you are being asked a goal-oriented question, then better student graduation rates will be your answer for this one because it is a SMART goal.

USING SMART GOALS

Let's look at a multiple choice question centered around SMART goals.

It is asking you about a SMART goal: So, goals that are Specific, Measurable, Action-Oriented, Realistic, and Timely. Depending on where you look, Action-Oriented may be replaced with Attainable and Timely may be replaces with Time-Bound, but it all means the same thing (you take actions to attain it and it has a time limit to be accomplished by a certain time). They gave you four goals to match with these.

The question says that a school leader is setting goals for students' success in reading and wants to include all important dimensions of goal setting. It then asks you to match each defined goal with the dimension of goal setting it best exemplifies. This question could be a drag and drop question where you drag the dimension to the specific part of the SMART goal (which is timely, which is specific, which is realistic, etc.).

So, we have four choices:

1. Students' comprehension skills will improve by the end of the second nine weeks,
2. Students will score a level three or higher on the ELA benchmark test,
3. Students' comprehension skills will improve by participating in the SRA reading program, and
4. 80% of students will pass the ELA benchmark test.

In my opinion, this is one of the most difficult questions you might get asked. Initially, I thought it would be a simple question to answer; however, as it is a "right or wrong" type question, it is more complicated than it looks. And the first time I tried this practice question, I definitely got it wrong! So to answer this, you will put 1, 2, 3, and 4 into the categories of Specific, Measurable, Realistic and attainable (action-oriented), and Time-bound (timely). You may want to write these out so you can answer the question before moving forward to the answer. TRY IT YOURSELF NOW BEFORE MOVING ON. DON'T PEEK.

Let's take a look at this. Anytime you see a question like this, the way to tackle it is to do the easiest one first.

The answer that relates to being time-bound is usually going to be your easy one, so look for an answer that has a time limit. That is to say, look for one of the answers that has a date, or which one of them has something to do with time or is related to time specifics.

If you look at the above example, there is only one of the answers that has to do with that, which is the first one: **1) Students' comprehension skills will improve by the end of the second nine weeks.**

This first answer is the only one that actually gives you a specific timeframe. Then it gets a little bit more difficult. So, we still have our realistic and attainable, measurable, and specific goals. Let's cover "specific" next.

Look at answers two, three, and four. Which one of these is the most specific and gives me the most details? Which one answers more question of who, what, why, where and when? This will be my specific answer. Number two states that students will score a level three or higher on the ELA benchmark test, number three states students' comprehension skills will improve by participating in the SRA program, and number four states that 80% of students will pass the ELA benchmark test.

I'm now looking at those three answers, and I'm looking for which one tells me what's going to happen and how it's going to happen. So, in this case, the answer that has this relevant information is going to be number three – which relates to students' comprehension skills.

I know we are talking about students (who), comprehension skills will improve (what) by participating in the SRA program (how). This is the only answer that tells me HOW we are going to accomplish the goal and gives me the most details. They purposely left off the when so you would not confuse this with the time-bound answer.

So we have our "time-bound" and "specific" answers. Now, it gets a little more difficult looking at "measurable," and "realistic"' and "attainable."

If I look at something to be "measurable," that means looking for something that has a measure point. So, I can say a score of level three or higher is a measure point, which is featured in answer two.

I could also say that the answer which mentions "80% of students" is a measure point, which it states in answer four. This is an example where I would have to delve a little deeper with data.

Measuring something, which one of those answers states "level 3 or higher," or "80% of students will pass," is, for want of a better word, specific. It is specific to measure, but I need to know which one of these actually reveals itself to be an actually measurement...which can I actually use as a specific measurement of achievement.

Can I truly measure "80% of students will pass?" How many students do I have? What is passing? Will they pass with certain scores? Can I truly measure "students will score a level three of higher?" I know I am looking at all the level 3 or higher scores. I can definitively say we have 10 students who scored level 3 or higher no mater how many students we have, I can grab a specific measurement from that and therefore, we have our answer!

The answer that contains "level three or higher" is the one that is going to give you what the actual measure is, versus just saying "80% of students," which is the vaguer of the two, and certainly not as measurable.

Answer number two here gives you a specific measure, as it shows the students are going to score the ELA benchmark tests at a level three or higher. So, that is how I would know that goal in question is being met.

Even though the difference may not appear clear-cut, when you consider all the above, this is how you can see that answer number two edges out and beats answer number four.

Moving from measurable, you also need to see if they are realistic and attainable. If it is a benchmark test, you would hope that most of your students will pass. Also, of course, process of elimination since it is the last answer left.

A benchmark test is how a teacher sets their standards for a semester, or another timeframe, which may be a month, six weeks, or nine weeks.

Whenever a benchmark test is given, a teacher is looking to see if their students meet those standards. It is formative, but also a kind of summative data set too.

Therefore, if a teacher is teaching the curriculum, then gives a benchmark test, it is very realistic and attainable that most of the students should pass it. So, you can see here, that's where the 80% of students passing the SLA benchmark test comes from.

This is definitely one of the toughest types of questions you may get asked, but if you understand well what each part of a SMART goal is for, you'll easily be able to answer any question of this nature that you are faced with.

10

CULTURAL RESPONSIVENESS AND PROGRAM IMPLEMENTATION

*I*n the last chapter, we looked at SMART goals, and now we're going to explore two other fundamental parts of educational leadership in the form of cultural responsiveness and program implementation.

DEFINING CULTURALLY RESPONSIVE PEDAGOGY

Working in the education field, you are likely to already know that the word "pedagogy" essentially means teaching, or more

specifically, teaching methodology. So, let's directly swap the words and replace "pedagogy" with the word "teaching," and now ask ourselves the question: What is *culturally responsive* teaching?

The best way to to begin to understand it is as a very student-centered approach to teaching. It is about using students' cultural strengths to promote student achievement.

Contrary to what clichés may be misunderstood about it, culturally responsive pedagogy is not about holding hands and singing Kumbaya in a circle!

It's really about student achievement, but by connecting the lesson and content to students' lives. It is about making your teaching relevant to your students because you are linking it to their lives, to their cultures, and to what they find valuable and important. .

WAYS TO MAKE PEDAGOGY CULTURALLY RESPONSIVE

One way to make teaching culturally responsive is to **establish inclusion**. This means making sure that not only the students, but also the teachers, feel respected and connected to one another.

Developing attitude is another method to make teaching culturally responsive. This is when you take the learning experience and make it personally relevant to your students. You really can only do this by knowing the students and giving students a choice and celebrating their voice in their own learning. This would mean providing instruction whereby students do something not just because they're told to, but because they have some agency in it – they're participating by making choices.

Enhancing meaning is when you take your content and view it through students' perspectives and values. So, you are connecting your content to the students' lives.

One of the worst questions any teacher can get is, "why are we learning this," or "how is what we're learning going to help me." This can be a bit of a conundrum for a teacher.

However, you should realize that students, in this case, are essentially asking what the point in the learning is. Fundamentally, they want to know what the content is bringing to their life that is going to contribute to making them a better person.

This is where enhancing the meaning comes into force. This is where you need to connect the learning experience to their life, and this means that you must connect it to their values.

There is also **engendering competence**. This is the concept that people learn what they see value in. So, for example, you are valuing this book right now and appreciate the learning experience because you need it as it is something that you value now – you realize that it is going to help you with your future goal.

If I would've given you the same book at the beginning of your career, it may not have been as much of a learning experience for you because it may not have been something you valued as much at that time.

In order for learning experiences to work, all students must understand and recognize why they're there. They need to know what it is that connects them to the learning and why it's important, and in this way, they will value it more. The more they see themselves and their culture validated through content, the more likely they are to be invested in the learning.

CULTURALLY RESPONSIVE CLASSROOMS

To create culturally responsive classrooms, there are some things that a leader can do.

Number one is to have teachers check their own biases. Not every person is a racist or a bigot, but every single person has a bias. Once we can consider what our biases are, we can begin to chip away at them. Once we know better, we can do better. After checking what are biases are, we also must understand B.D.A. How do our Biases Determine our Actions? We need to ask ourselves how we are treating our students, parents, and co-workers differently because those biases seep in to our actions. Again, once we start doing this work on ourselves, which is not easy or comfortable, we can begin to heal, apologize for our actions and begin to not make the same mistakes again.

Number two is making sure that teachers are are open to learning about your students' cultures and what their interests are. If you do not KNOW your students, you cannot CONNECT to your students. As the great Rita Pierson once said, "Kids don't learn from people they don't like." I would add students don't learn from people who don't know or understand them as people first and students second. Helping your teachers understand this is key to creating culturally responsive classrooms.

Number three is that it is necessary to make sure teachers' classrooms are brave spaces. Classrooms should be a place where students can actually say their opinions without judgment. Whether viewed as right or wrong by a majority, just having that space to bravely speak, amplify voices, and discuss opinions is a crucial thing for a classroom environment.

And finally, number four is to ensure your teachers understand how to teach, and are teaching, in a culturally responsive way.

PROGRAM IMPLEMENTATION

Program implementation is not about planning the talent show or assemblies. What is meant by program implementation is anything that you are implementing throughout instruction and systems on campus.

This could be something with curriculum, or it could be on a bell schedule, or it could be a Positive Behavioral Interventions and Supports (PBIS) program. Essentially, it is anything that will have an effect on your school or department.

For example, if you implement a new lunch schedule at your school, what would you need to do? The following are the steps to take when implementing any program.

To begin, you would need to get stakeholder input, which may involve forming a committee. You would never make a decision by yourself, as everything is about getting stakeholder input and buy-in. So, because stakeholder input is a must, your only decision is whose input is needed and how to gather the information.

You may be asking who is considered a stakeholder. A stakeholder is anyone who has a stake in your school or department succeeding. For a school, that would be the students, teachers, administration, cafeteria staff, custodians, nurse, library media specialist, paraprofessionals, counselor, office staff (all adults on campus), parents, siblings/families, the district, community businesses, residents of the community, feeder schools, etc. Anyone who wants to see your students succeed. Even if I am a retiree in the neighborhood and don't have any students at the school, I still want you to teach them to not break into my home and to be productive members of society and to make money to spend in the community and to take care of the community. So I have a stake in you succeeding and am therefore, a stakeholder. That doesn't mean I need to take a part in all your decision making, but only the areas that make sense.

You may not ever see the "S" word (stakeholder) in the question, but you will see an answer that states something like, "forming a committee," which implies stakeholder inclusion. You may also see an answer that says something like, "bring together the science teachers, the parents," etc. Remember that it might not say the word "stakeholder," but the action will be you forming a committee, and, therefore, that would be a strong answer to consider.

DATA

The second thing you will consider is data and trends for the program.

If you do not have data to support why the program needs to be implemented, then why are you implementing the program?

Let's go back to the example of changing the lunch schedule. First, you have included stakeholders. Now, you, with your stakeholders, are going to look at the data to show the reasons why you're changing the lunch schedule.

The data you would need to review include how the lunch schedule looked before, asking whether there are any issues, and whether the new program is going to solve your problems.

What you are doing here is looking at your own school's data to see if implementing the program will solve your problems. The next step in program implementation is to look at comparative data from similar schools.

For example, if you are in a high school with 1800 students with 50% white, 50% black, and 20% free and reduced lunch.

What you would ideally be doing is looking at the data from a similar school that has been successful in implementing a similar program to what you now intend to launch, see what they did, and then get advice.

For the data to work, it would need to be comparative. So, a middle school with 80% white, 20% black, and 90% free and reduced lunch would not work. That school does not have the same issue as yours, so you are not going to have the same successes or problems.

Therefore, you would need to find a school similar to yours. That school could be out of your district or even out of your state. The most important thing is that you would need to find a school with similar demographics, and then look at their results as a comparison.

The next step in program implementation is to get additional input. So, bring the committee back together and do some more research on the program and implementation. If we need to gather more original data at that point, then do so.

PLAN AND PROGRESS MONITOR

The penultimate step in this is that you would need to plan your implementation effectively. You would not want to start your new program haphazardly, and careful planning is required. For example, things you would need to plan for in the implementation might include the timetabling and phases of implementation.

Lastly, you would need to implement the program and monitor the progress. This might mean that as part of your program implementation, for the progress monitoring, you might have teachers meet once a week during their planning period and get them to bring data and student work to see what kind of effect this new program is having on your students.

11

LEADERSHIP STYLES

This chapter will cover leadership styles, which is something that appears in the multiple choice part of the test.

LEADERSHIP STYLES

There are many different leadership styles, but here are seven that you need to know, as well as their benefits and drawbacks.

1. Authoritarian (a.k.a. autocratic). Authoritarian/autocratic is the leadership style that rarely accepts advice from others. This type of leader makes all the decisions based on their own ideas.

The *benefit* of this approach is a leader can accomplish a lot in a little time. Essentially, this is because the leaders are just telling people what to do. For example, in a faculty meeting, you can quickly tell staff what they need to do and dismiss them with no discussion or feedback. The leader is able to distribute great amounts of information quickly.

The *drawback* is that this can lead to a lack of commitment. Staff may be carrying out your instructions, but because they did not have agency in the decision, they don't necessarily feel committed to it. On this test, authoritarian/autocratic leadership style is not a positive approach. In fact, this is the most negative approach that you could take as a leader, according to the test.

2. Democratic is, in many ways, the opposite of authoritarian, as consensus is sought, rather than just giving orders to be followed.

The *benefit* of being democratic is that a leader gains a high level of commitment from their staff. With this leadership style, the group makes the decision collectively. Therefore, all staff involved in the decision-making had agency. Even if they did not get their preference selected, they were still a part of the decision-making process, which instills a greater commitment to achieving the goals of the decision. And so, the democratic way of leadership gains a high level of commitment because staff had their say in making the decision, whether they agreed with the final outcome or not.

The *drawback* to this leadership style is that because the decisions are made in a group dynamic, there could be a lack of actual leadership. Rather than having one person in control, everyone is in control, making it hard for people to take on certain responsibilities. Since there is no defined leader in the decision-making process, people may not feel as responsible for achieving any of the goals of the decision. On the test, the democratic leadership style is the best approach as this means that you are getting stakeholder input, and you are also getting other people involved, which is what they are looking for.

3. Distributive. This means that the leader distributes leadership roles to others.

The *benefit* of a distributive leader is the leader builds their people up since they allow other people to take leadership roles. For example, if a leader asks their assistant principal to ensure all IEPs are properly written and signed, they are distributing that leadership role. By doing this, they are edifying their staff.

Now, there could be two *drawbacks* to this. One drawback is personal. A leader actually has to allow their staff to lead for it to work. The leader cannot be a micromanager and a distributive leader. When they give their staff that role, they must actually give them the authority to do the role.

The second **drawback** may be one of a technical issue for the situation. Whoever the leader distributes a task to actually must know how to carry out whatever role they are being given. So, if a leader gives their assistant principal the task of carrying out the individual education plans (IEPs), the leader needs to make sure that the individual person actually knows how to do it and cannot just assume. Therefore, a distributive leader can only give roles that make sense to their staff skills-wise, which is certainly a drawback to consider with this type of leadership style, as it may not always be possible to apply it.

4. Transformative. These kinds of leaders are the ones that you see movies about! These are your charismatic leaders; these are your life changers.

So, the *benefit* of the transformative leadership style is that the leader creates the type of change that positively changes lives. These are the individuals that books are written about, and movies are based upon. They reformulate the lives of the teachers and students on their campuses in a way that makes the community and world at large take notice.

The *drawback* is that with this leadership style, if the leaders don't build their people up, or if they don't teach their people how to do what they can do, then the transformation leaves with them. Even though it sounds ideal, it is hard to keep that momentum going. If you are not that kind of person, if you are not that transformative leader, then it's hard to keep that momentum going once that transformative leader leaves. So, you must build up your people and create that really strong foundation.

5. Situational. This is the leader that adjusts their leadership style depending on the group.

The main *benefit* of adopting this approach is that a leader adapts themselves depending on the situation. This pretty much makes it a nice hybrid of all the other leadership styles. If the staff needs a transformative leader, then the situational leader can become that person at the time. If the staff need to have roles distributed, then the leader can adapt to this, too, at the time. That is what a situational leader does, which is the main *benefit.*

The *drawback* to this leadership style is that a leader absolutely must know their staff. They have to be able to get the right approach with the right person. If they do not find this equilibrium, the leader will start turning the staff off. For example, if in one instance a leader comes across as an authoritarian leader but then comes across as a democratic leader in another instance, this will alienate the staff–you could see the dangers of inconsistency here. Also, in real life, I like an autocratic leader. Just tell me what you need and leave me to it. If I want to discuss it, I will come to you. But, if the situational leaders always approaches me with the democratic style (because he doesn't know my preference), he will alienate me. So, all in all, a situational leader has to know their people.

6. Systematic. The definition of a systematic leader is someone who follows the system – point blank, period. For a systematic leader, rules are the rules, and that is that. For them, the system is the system. Systematic leaders are very policy-driven.

The *benefit* of being a systematic leader is that it does remove bias. It is very effective, and no one is going to say that the leader favors one person over another person, because the leader is ensuring that the same policy is followed by all, no matter what.

The *drawback* to this style of leadership, as you may be guessing by now, is that this rigid approach also removes common sense and emotional awareness. It eliminates the human element.

Let's look at an example. Ms. Smith comes in 5 minutes late. She has a McDonald's bag and McDonald's cup in her hand. The principal looks at her and says, "I'm docking you for 5 minutes." Then, Mr. Tom comes in right behind her. He has blood on his face and glass in his hair. The principal looks at him and says, "I am docking you for 5 minutes."

As you can see, in this case, Mr. Tom has probably been in a car accident, but Ms. Smith was late only because she wanted to grab a McMuffin before work. So, obviously, they do not have the same situation going on, yet the principal still docked them both 5 minutes' pay, according to the rules of the system. The systematic leader followed a systematic approach.

Any observers cannot say that the principal favored one teacher over the other in this situation, as they are both getting reprimanded equally. However, given the scenario, it would make sense to show empathy to Mr. Tom and not punish him for being 5 minutes late in the same way as someone who went to McDonald's.

In the above example, common sense would tell you that there are different situations at play here that would need to be reacted to differently, and this is why being a purely systematic leader isn't always the best.

7. Shared Leadership. This leadership style is very closely related to distributive leadership as this leader gives others leadership roles. However, they also ensure that multiple people on the campus/in the department are involved in the decision making.

The *benefit* is the leader is not running everything by themselves. Instead, the leader is making sure that multiple people on the campus are involved in the decision-making, and that they also have leadership roles. Many campuses these days have shared leadership styles in thatyou have your mentor teachers, your teacher leaders, the head of the English Department, and other leader roles like that.

The *drawbacks* are the same as with a distributive leader.

A question that asks about a shared leadership style may give you a scenario that involves a shared leader, so you need to know how to recognize it.

Mr. Smith has this specific issue and he uses a shared leadership style. How would he respond?

He would need to respond by getting the input of others. He would need to give other people leadership roles and decision-making roles on this issue.

KNOWING YOUR LEADERSHIP STYLES

There are seven main leadership styles that you need to know to answer questions in the SLLA 6990 test: Authoritarian/Autocratic, Democratic, Distributive, Transformative, Situational, Systematic, and Shared.

12
DATA

This chapter is all about data and will start by giving you definitions of types of data, followed by how you can examine the data. You will learn what validity and reliability are, and also what authentic data means.

There will also be a focus on the difference between qualitative and quantitative data. Additionally, the meanings of grade equivalency and aggregated data will be discussed, as well as taking you through what percentiles and normative groups mean.

As you can see, there are several definitions and concepts to take on board when it comes to understanding how to use data and linking this to the questions that will arise on the SLLA 6990 test, so you may want to really slow down and absorb the information presented in this chapter, re-reading the paragraphs if necessary. Let's start with data definitions and then continue from there.

DATA DEFINITIONS

Formative data shows progress, such as weekly tests for teachers or walkthroughs for leaders. It is simply to see what progress is being made. For example, a teacher may issue an end-of-week test on a Friday to see what students have picked up from the week, and then from this, the teacher can judge what may need to be covered again if there is a trend that implies many students missed the knowledge. The teacher would be checking on what progress the students made in that week. It is not long-term, but just to check on the progress being made.

An administrator may want to know how a teacher is making progress by completing a walkthrough.

Rather than waiting until the end of the learning module, an administrator can check in with a teacher along the way and collect data about their progress, and see if they have implemented any of the improvements that were suggested to them.

Summative data is the summary of the end of a learning period, so that could be a semester or the entire year.

So, for a teacher, summative data could be gained from the results of an end-of-year exam, or the final exam. For an administrator, that could be that last, final meeting that they have with the teacher where they go over all their observations and give them their score for the year.

Formal / Informal. Formal data is any data that is written down, whereas informal data is any data that is not written down. For example, if an administrator does a walkthrough and they do not write down data, they still witnessed that data. They may have not written it down, but it is still data – it is *informal* data. If an administrator does that same walkthrough using a rubric, the data is now formalized – it is *formal* data.

Criterion and Normative. You may see criterion featured often on the test. Criterion is all about content. Think about the "C" for criterion and the "C" for content. This is your content test, which is a test that just wants to see whether a student knows the content. It is not comparing the student to other students. It is just asking the student whether they know the content.

The SLLA test that you are about to take is, in fact, a criterion test. It is asking if you know how to handle these situations and if you know the content. When you get your scores, it will not compare you to other test takers. It will just give you your scores according to whether you know the content.

For normative, think about the "N" from normative as in nationwide. This is the test where students are being compared to other equivalent students, usually nationwide. This is more like your ACT test, where they tell students that they are within a percentile of other people that have taken the same test, which makes it a normative assessment (nationwide comparison).

Validity and Reliability. When you are trying to see if your data is valid, you are going to ask these two questions: 1) Is this the right test? 2) Am I measuring the right thing? Both of these are how you can tell if your data has validity.

For reliability, you're going to ask these two questions: 1) Are we assessing everyone in the same way? 2) Are we grading in the same way?

If I did a walkthrough for one person, but then a formal observation for another person, and then compared that data, this is not reliable as I did not assess both in the same way. Also, if I have a rubric when performing a walkthrough that asks questions about a teacher's instruction, but bases it on how clean her classroom is, that would not be valid data because I am not measuring the right thing.

Authentic Data. This is your *real-world* application. In other words, are you actually using what was taught. For a leader, this would be seeing if a teacher actually incorporated some of the strategies discussed in the actual lesson.

Quantitative and Qualitative. These are two sides of a coin when it comes to data. Quantitative is hard data, the numbers. So, you could think of the "N" in qua-N-titative and numbers.

Quantitative data is numbers, so it could be test scores or it could be attendance records.

In fact, when we talk about data, most of us instinctively only think about the quantitative form.

However, the other type of data can be just as useful. Qua-Li-tative with the "L." That's soft data. This is all the kind of data that can be gathered which is not numerical. This could involve collating people's opinions or feelings on topics from surveys, interviews, or observations.

However, the thing to remember is that all qualitative data can be taken and made quantitative. Anything can be quantified. For example, you could take a walkthrough and then say how many times something was observed, and this then makes it quantitative.

Grade Equivalency. Let's take an example using grade equivalency. Let's use the number 3.5. What does that mean?

If I say that Johnny's grade equivalency is 3.5, the first number is the grade level year. So, Johnny is in third grade. The second number, 0.5, is how many months that child has been in that grade level.

Therefore, if I say Johnny has a 3.5, that means that Johnny is in the fifth month of his third-grade year.

Now, where grade equivalency comes into use is when I say that Johnny is a fourth-grade student dealing with spring testing. So, that would mean Johnny should be at a 4.7 or 4.8 grade equivalency. If Johnny's grade equivalency is a 3.5, we know that he is below grade level.

Because this test is nationwide, some students start in August, and some start school in September. However, it does not matter when a student starts school.

Usually, spring testing is around two months before the school year ends. So, this indicates that Johnny should be at 4.7 or 4.8.

However, we know that he is actually at 3.5, so now we can say that Johnny is definitely behind where he should be for his grade level.

Using this example, that is how you use grade equivalency. In the constructed response section of this book, we are going to look at a data table and then break that down into more detail.

Understanding grade equivalency now is really going to help us later.

Aggregated Data. "Aggregated" is one of the most misused words in education. I will also tell you the second-most misused words later, but in my opinion, this is the first most misused word in education.

Aggregating data means gathering different data points, and then putting them together to create a statistical analysis. But there is a difference between aggregating data and evaluating it. Evaluating data is reviewing the data and coming to a conclusion. For aggregation to occur, you must have multiple data points that work together to create your analysis.

If I take the third-grade test scores, free and reduced lunch status, and the attendance records, then I take all three of those data points and put them together to create an analysis, that is aggregating the data.

What you could find from the data aggregation is some trends, such as when looking at these three data points and you see that when our students who are on free and reduced lunch missed more than five days, they also dropped 20% on the standardized test.

Making a statistical analysis in this way is aggregating the data. You can also draw conclusions from your analysis and make decisions and interventions from it.

For example, from the same analysis, you could then say that if they are on free and reduced lunch and miss day three, we need to have some interventions. This is because we can assume (according to the data) that if they miss two days or more, their scores are about to decrease on the test.

Percentile Definition. This would be the percentage of how many are *below* the number you are looking at. The idea of what a percentile is can sometimes be a little tricky to comprehend, as it is not the number but whatever is below that number.

As an example, if I tell you that you are in the national 20th percentile, that means 20% of the nation is below where you are.

So, let's look at it a little bit deeper. If I said that you are in the 20th percentile of people scoring on the SLLA test, is this effectively a good or bad thing? Well, that means that 20% of the test-takers nationwide received a lower score than you.

You can flip it around because that also means that 80% of the test-takers nationwide scored higher than you. In other words, that is negative because only 20% scored lower, so 20% of the rest of the people in the United States who took this test scored lower than what you did – and 80% scored higher. Sometimes it helps to flip it to really understand it.

Also, do not be tricked into thinking that the higher the percentile, the better it is because this depends on the category in question. For example, if you are talking about a test, then yes, the higher the percentile, the better. If a person meets the 90th percentile of people who took this test, then yes, that is good. It means that only 10% scored higher than a person. That is definitely an achievement.

However, in another category, scoring high in the percentile might be a bad thing. For example, let's talk about weight. If someone is in the 80th percentile of weight, that isn't good. That means 80% of people are below that person's weight; in other words, only 20% of people are heavier than they are.

Hopefully, you can see now how percentiles work and whether being in the higher or lower percentile is essentially a good or bad thing, depending on the category. Usually, though, for student test scores, the higher, the better.

Norm Group or Normative Group. As a definition, these are the sample of test-takers who are representatives of the population for whom the test was intended. I know...what?

Let's use an example. There are 1800 students at a high school, and you want to give them a survey to get an overall representation of the student body, but you do not want to survey all 1800 students because you don't have the time or the resources to process all of the surveys, particularly as you have an impending deadline.

What you would then do is choose a norm group to survey. That means you would get together representatives of the student population for whom the survey was intended. In this case, the survey was intended for all 1800 students, and so in order to get a norm group, you must break them down into whatever category is important to your survey.

Therefore, how you create your norm group would depend on what you are surveying. But, let's say you choose to break it down by those who are on free and reduced lunch, by racial category, by grade level, by sexual orientation, by test scores, or any other distinction that would be able to create a sample of the wider body of students.

Let's say that the high school consists of 50% Asian students and 50% Latinx students, and just for the sake of brevity, there are only two races. Also, 80% of the students are on free and reduced lunch. Further, there are 20% boys, and 80% girls.

What you would then do is put all of those populations into your sample group. Since the population is 80% girls and 20% boys, you would need to have more girls in the norm group (80% of the number in your norm group), because girls represent a higher part of the population.

The main thing is that you get the correct proportion and representation of all the groups of your wider student population into your sample, your norm group.

Some do not agree with the use of norm groups. For example, they feel that one Native Hawaiian/Pacific Islander female student cannot represent or speak for all Native Hawaiian/Pacific Islander female students at the school. However, for this example, the thought process behind normative groups is ensuring that Native Hawaiian/Pacific Islander female students have a representation on the survey.

A norm group is useful for reducing time and costs associated with surveying entire populations. Using norm groups is a tried and tested method for all sorts of market research and polling, and can be equally applied to data collection in your own school.

PIECING IT ALL TOGETHER

Having gone through all the definitions of the different data terminology, hopefully, you will now have a better idea of what to expect when it comes to answering data questions that may come up on the multiple choice section of the SLLA 6990.

It is important that you understand these key concepts and definitions, so if there is anything you're unsure of, please take the time to re-read the sections you are still unsure of before moving on to the next chapter, which is about supporting teachers and rigor.

13

SUPPORTING TEACHERS AND RIGOR

ou're more than halfway through this part of the book, which is a guide on what to expect in the multiple choice section of the SLLA 6990 test.

This chapter is about how to support teachers. It will cover how you can support new teachers and more experienced, veteran teachers. This chapter will also provide advice on how to create rigorous curriculum and classrooms and how curriculum mapping ties into them both.

NEW TEACHERS

As an educational leader, the test is naturally going to ask you questions about how you would support your teachers and staff. One obvious place to start is how you can provide support to new and inexperienced teachers.

When you see the word "new" on the test, this is an indication that it is time to put your warm and fuzzy hat on!

This means that you must never reprimand a new teacher. It does not matter what the new teacher is doing, whether right or wrong. The main thing is you never reprimand them and only commit to actions that support them.

When it comes to processes and techniques, as a leader, you always need to be supporting any new teachers. There are various ways you can support them, but one tried and tested method is to provide them with a mentor.

You can also provide structured support by setting up times for them to meet with you, as well as provide other training such as arranging for them to do observations of classes taught by more experienced teachers.

There may be many other similar support options for new teachers, but whatever you need to do, if it says the word "new" in that question, the answer will not be anything that mentions reprimanding them and will always be the more supportive, caring and helpful action step.

VETERAN TEACHERS

First of all, let's clarify the terminology. Sometimes on the test, they will use the word "veteran" for more experienced teachers; at other times, they will just say "teacher."

If you see the word "teacher" alone, you can assume that they are not referring to new teachers, but the more experienced teachers who have been around longer.

Nevertheless, even with more experienced teachers, your approach is still going to be that you are going to talk to them first about any issues. Your first priority is that you still want to support them and provide them with the help that they need.

However, if the question states that the veteran teacher is consistently making the wrong decision or consistently doing something that they should not be doing (especially after having been supported first), then you can reprimand them for purposes of responding on this test.

The correct answer in these situations that refers to more experienced teachers who have previously been supported but are still making the same mistakes would be to reprimand them officially, which might entail putting them on a corrective action plan or a similar strategy.

MENTOR TEACHERS

With both novice and experienced teachers, the first action would be to provide support first, and this may include setting up a mentor for them. This is why you are likely to get questions that ask you how you're going to choose teachers to be mentors.

When it asks you this, you will select mentor teachers from those willing to help. It is important that you choose people who have a heart to help.

You would not choose mentor teachers from those who teach the same content, teach in the classroom close to the teacher who needs help, or the teacher who has been there the longest. You are going to choose those that volunteer to help.

We touched on this in a previous chapter, but let's say one of the teachers is having problems with the students, and the mentor teacher tries to help, but the teacher is still having problems with the students. What should the mentor do?

The answer here would be that the mentor needs to recommend the teacher in question comes to you for further guidance. As a school leader, you are the head disciplinarian on that campus. Just because you have assigned a mentor that does not mean you do not have any responsibility to deal with the problem directly. You are not untouchable, and staff still need to come and talk to you to resolve problems.

RIGOROUS CURRICULUM

I told you I would tell you my opinion for the second most misused word in education, and here it is: rigor.

In everyday life, the term "rigor" or "rigorous" may mean difficult. However, if we are talking about curriculum, it means something different and quite specific.

When using the word rigorous to refer to curriculum, it does not mean "difficult," but it means that the curriculum is strictly aligned with state and national standards.

When we talk about a rigorous curriculum, especially on this test, it means aligned to the state and national standards. So, you may see a question that asks something like, "Ms. Smith's class all makes A's and B's on their report cards. Ms. Smith is an awesome teacher. All of her students are on the honor roll. But, when Ms. Smith's students took the benchmark test, over half of them fail it. What is the problem?"

Essentially, the problem here is that Ms. Smith is not teaching a rigorous curriculum. The content she is teaching in her class is not based on the curriculum and that is why her students are all on the honor roll. But, when those same students try to take the benchmark which is based directly from the curriculum, they fail it. If they failed the benchmark, they should be failing Ms. Smith's class if they are both based from the curriculum.

RIGOROUS CLASSROOM

As featured above, a rigorous *curriculum* ensures that the curriculum is actually aligned to the state national standards. A rigorous *classroom* makes sure that the students are actually engaged in the lesson that follows a curriculum that is aligned to the state and national standards.

So, to take this in context, a rigorous classroom is where students make meaning for themselves. They need to understand why it is important for them to be learning the lesson; this also ties in with culturally responsive teaching.

By understanding just why the lesson is important to them, the students are imposing structure on the information. A rigorous classroom means students learn how to organize information/impose structure to the information in a way that makes sense to them. The thought behind this is to have your students analyze what are the systems that help them learn the best.

The next aspect of a rigorous classroom is allowing students to take what they previously have learned and what they currently are learning and create processes with their knowledge.

It is not simply a case of rote learning, or the students being able to say that they've learned step one, and now they will go ahead and learn step two, then step three, and that's it. Instead, it is about creating something from it.

The students ought to take all the individual skills that they have just learned and then put them together to solve a problem. In this case, a problem need not be a true problem, but parts that make up a whole to create something else. Then, to further their knowledge, ask how they can apply it to other issues and problems and how can they make other solutions with their knowledge (and possibly what else they need to learn to do so). By doing this, you are taking learning to whole new level for students and creating that rigorous classroom.

By this time, you may be thinking why are we discussing all of these things to do in the classroom when this is a leadership test. Well, remember, as an educational leader, you are the instructional leader of that school. If you do not know how classrooms should look and what should be happening in them, how will you help any teachers with their instruction? Also remember that instructional leadership is one of the main focuses on this test whether your goal is to be a campus leader or not.

CURRICULUM MAPPING ALIGNMENT

You may have heard the term "curriculum mapping" before, where you ensure that the curriculum is mapped (aligned) to the standards. However, while you are mapping your curriculum, you also have to consider the two types of alignments: horizontal and vertical.

Horizontal alignment is curricular alignment within a common grade level (same content is being taught among the same grade level in every classroom and is aligned to state and national standards) to ensure students are adequately prepared for the next level as well as grade level assessments. This provides teachers/faculty within the same grade level a guide and goals for instruction.

Vertical alignment is cross-institutional or cross-grade level ensuring content students learn in a lower grade level or course prepares them for the next grade level or course and content is aligned to the state or national standards. This will help students transition successfully to the next level. So, for example, you can have the fifth-grade teachers at the elementary school collaborate with the sixth-grade teachers at the middle school to analyze curriculums and student data to conclude what parts of the curriculum are being taught, which are not, and how is it affecting students. Then, plans could be made about what to focus on in fifth grade to support students going to sixth grade. Because this collaboration is being done between two different grade levels and campuses, it would be vertical alignment.

Vertical alignment encompasses curriculum mapping across different grade levels and possibly across the different schools, whereas with horizontal alignment, you are keeping it in the same school and at the same grade level.

Make sure that you know the difference between the two so that you do not get caught off guard when the test asks you about vertical alignment vs. horizontal alignment. These questions may come up when they ask about professional development, too, which is in the next chapter of this book.

BRINGING IT ALL TOGETHER: SUPPORTING TEACHERS AND RIGOR

This chapter covered two sides of a coin: Supporting teachers and providing rigor. When it comes to supporting teachers, we looked at ways to support new and veteran teachers and how to select mentors.

Related to this is how you can provide rigor – in the curriculum and in the classroom. This is so that your school can function effectively and teachers are doing what they can to ensure that students are passing their assessments.

Finally, we explored the idea of curriculum mapping alignment. There are two kinds of alignment you can do with curriculum mapping – horizontal and vertical. Make sure you know which is which.

14

PROFESSIONAL DEVELOPMENT

*P*rofessional development (commonly abbreviated to PD) is something you often hear when it comes to leadership in education. This is because teachers need to be learners themselves.

Teachers (and educational leaders) are meant never to stop learning, and professional development plans provide the path for them to excel. PD plans for teachers should be full of ideas that help make them the best teachers they can be, with access to the relevant places to grow and learn.

In this slightly shorter chapter, we will focus on professional development plans and see how educational leaders can use them.

WHAT SHOULD PROFESSIONAL DEVELOPMENT BE?

Despite certain misconceptions, PD must be research-based. You should have research and data to support why certain PD offerings are chosen over others. It should not be as simple as *I went to a conference and thought this was great*. That's nice, but we should be asking how will this PD specifically help our campus, what are the goals for the PD, what should we be implementing after the PD, and how will this implementation positively affect teacher growth which in turn will positively affect student achievement.

Also, PD must be ongoing. No aspect of PD should be isolated; it should be ongoing, going from one level to the next, perhaps including other aspects such as project-based learning.

If a person is learning a skill, they should be learning different things about that same skill in an ongoing fashion. Perhaps they need to take it up a level, or learn how to practically use it in different contents or situations. The PD should not be one and done.

It also needs to be modeled, as there should be somebody either on the campus or in the district who can model the PD in the situation where it should be used. This gives teachers time to consider how this will actually look in their own classrooms. For example, I should be able to go and see your classroom and then see a teacher successfully implementing what we learned in PD in a classroom setting with real students.

Finally, it needs to be progress monitored. Something should not be put into place in September and then not checked until May! You would not want to waste an entire academic year on something that wasn't working. Progress monitoring is important to make sure the PD is beneficial.

EMBEDDED PROFESSIONAL DEVELOPMENT

You may get a question on the test that asks you about the best way to implement PD, which will be called "embedded professional development."

There may be different names for it, such as "train the trainer," but the main idea behind this is having those key staff go and learn whatever skill it is, and then bring it back to teach it to the rest of the staff.

It has been shown that teachers respond better to PD from other teachers, who are their peers, especially from colleagues they trust.

You should never have a whole department going to a conference unless you are sure that each of them will be able to fully comprehend and soak up the learning experience of the event.

There is also job-embedded professional development, which is one of those hot terms now, and certainly is likely to appear on the test.

What this refers to is that teachers are learning in their environment, and about what they are actually doing in the classroom. It is not a case of what the teacher *wants* to do in the classroom, but it is actually what they're *already* doing in the classroom. They are learning content specific skills and strategies to make their daily instructional practices better for their current placement.

Oftentimes, this job-embedded PD is learning throughout the school day in the school or the classroom where the teacher is every day.

APPROACHING PROFESSIONAL DEVELOPMENT

As for the test, you need to know that PD is about the current work of schools and teachers. PD is about what teachers are doing in their roles and what they need or want to learn more regarding their content and specific instructional practices.

As an example, a math teacher needs to be learning about subject-specific content and instructional practices.

PD should not be generic training, and the math teacher ought to be learning about something they are specifically teaching at that present time. Also, the learning needs to be done on the job, in the school, and during the school day.

15

SPED, DISCIPLINE, CRISIS PLANS, HANDLING DEATHS AND BEREAVEMENTS

*T*his chapter will also focus on other things you'd need to manage as part of your role as a leader. Rather than separate them out, you can see that these themes are linked in terms of their people management across all staff and areas of the school.

This chapter starts with a focus on Special Education (SPED),

starting with some of the laws associated with it. The rest of the chapter will look at areas of Individualized Education Programs (IEPs) and response interventions when it comes to SPED.

There is then a more general look at how you would manage student discipline, crisis plans, and how to handle death and bereavement. You should make sure that you come to grips with the implications of each of these topics, as they are all likely to come up on the SLLA 6990 test.

SPED LAW

The SLLA 6990 test is not designed to test all knowledge of SPED law, but it will ask you things that you should know as an entry-level leader.

Here are some examples of information you should know for the test. If a teacher comes to you and tells you that one of their students needs to be tested for SPED, what are some questions you should ask that teacher?

Before doing anything else, the first thing you need to ask that teacher is what interventions they have tried with the student in question.

The second thing you need to ask is how long have these intervention measures been tried.

It is important to ask these questions because a student cannot be screened for SPED without getting parental approval and permission. So, if one of the answers is to automatically go and test that student, you already know that it is one of the wrong answers.

If the answer states that you have parental approval, then maybe that is the correct one, but an answer on the test that does not state that you already have the parental approval will be wrong.

You need to make sure that the teacher tries to help the student first before moving on to SPED testing. So, you must ask what interventions they tried. An intervention could be something as straightforward as placing the student at the front of the classroom.

The next question would be how long they tried that intervention. For example, if they say they tried it for a week and it did not work, that is not enough time for an intervention to be successful and change behavior. It is important to note interventions take from six to eight weeks to see if they work. The above example of the teacher only having tried it out for a week would not be considered long enough.

In addition, it would be helpful to look into what options parents have when they want to complain about SPED decisions, as this may be something else you're asked about on the test. You can start with this resource: bit.ly/sllaspedcomplaints

RESPONSE INTERVENTIONS

Response interventions have three tiers. A teacher would use whole group intervention with the entire class (tier 1). Then there is small group intervention (tier 2), and lastly, there is intensive intervention (tier 3) — a teacher's 1:1 response to intervention.

An IEP is a student's Individualized Education Plan. These are the plans that a teacher puts into place to help a student when they are in the SPED program.

The IEP will list what accommodations the student should have, as well as describing why they are in SPED, and also the measures put in place to help that student.

As a leader, you would be the one responsible for signing off on the IEP. This means you are the one to commit funding to that IEP. Therefore, when you put your signature on that IEP, you must make sure you have the funds.

If you agree to an IEP but later realize that you do not have the budget to commit to it, you risk dealing with losing federal funds. So, anything you sign on the IEP commits funding to it.

DISCIPLINE

Now, let's move on to another important area of SPED and discuss discipline. Anytime you deal with things like weapons, violence, drugs, drug paraphernalia, and so on, you want to consider the zero-tolerance policy.

For example, if the question says that you find a cigarette lighter or anything that could be considered a weapon, then your answer on the test will always be zero tolerance. Let's go through a quick example. A student (non-SPED) drove to school one morning, and someone reported to you that they saw a rifle in that student's car. You call the student in, and the student says, "I have no clue what you're talking about."

Then, things escalate. The parent comes to school, realizes what happened, and tells you, "Oh, my goodness. That is my rifle. I used my child's car over the weekend. We went hunting. I just completely forgot to take it out of the car. It's really not their fault. It's my fault."

In this example, what would you do? Some of your choices may be as follows: A) Recommend the student for suspension or expulsion according to district policy. B) Give that student a lesser sentence since the parent admitted fault. C) Give that student in-school suspension. D) No consequence since it was not the student's fault.

Zero-tolerance is still your answer because it involves weapons. A gun was brought on campus, and that is it. You cannot deviate from your zero-tolerance approach.

This is true, however, unless talking about a SPED student. You cannot do zero-tolerance with the SPED student if that means punishing that SPED student for behavior resulting from something in the student's IEP.

For example, if a student's IEP says that the student suffers from impulse control and they throw a book at the teacher's head, then that SPED student cannot be punished if that action resulted from the student's impulse control issues, as described in their IEP.

When it comes to SPED students, you cannot adopt the zero-tolerance approach, but you could have a manifestation determination review. From this type of review, you could see whether that action resulted from an issue that was already known in the IEP.

Something else important to note is that you cannot suspend a SPED student for more than ten days in a school year.

CRISIS PLANS

Four things must be included in any crisis plan: 1) mitigation and prevention, 2) preparedness, 3) response, and 4) recovery. Get a practice plan into place and look at some examples of crisis plans from other institutions.

With a crisis plan, you need to think carefully about who and what needs to be included in a crisis plan. When it comes to a crisis plan, everybody on that campus needs to be included in it. Crisis plans can cover a whole host of events, including fire drills, tornado drills, active shooter drills, or anything else that would present a crisis on your campus.

The crisis plan needs to include what to do and who it calls upon, what drills need to be put into place, and anything that would happen on your campus as a result of a crisis.

HANDLING DEATH AND BEREAVEMENT

Handling the death of a student is never easy and never something you can truly prepare for. But, as the educational leader, you must prepare as much as possible for such a tragic event.

Here are some ways that you can handle the death of the student. First, you would need to verify all the facts to make sure that you have all the correct information. The last thing you would want is a situation where rumors are running rampant, and you certainly would not want to become a part of that rumor mill unnecessarily.

Get the correct information and verify the facts. You then want to make sure that your faculty and staff know what is going on, and how it is being handled, as well as suggestions for handling it.

One of the things that you want to make sure of is that you have a crisis plan in place just for this occasion. The plan needs to make sure that there is an alert system that notifies staff, families, and students and duly informs them of the situation. Do not underestimate the impact of any student's or teacher's death on students and other faculty. Expect every death that might occur to have maximum impact on all staff and students.

You will need to give steps in the plan that include providing counselors to talk to students, and as part of this, you would need to allow time for students to work through the issues and provide the same to staff.

You will need to think about how you approach making the announcement of the news, considering how you might need to hold a meeting to inform staff and students, which could also be an opportunity to inform them what support is available.

Also, one of the big things to do when something like this happens is to contact your district media person, or if you operate as an individual campus, then whoever your campus media liaison person is. If you do not have one, then assign one, as the media is going to be asking for information. You can include details about who will be the relevant media liaison officer in your crisis plan.

When the media outlets find out about the news, they will want to do things like interview people and take pictures. They may want to be there with the counselors. So, you want to make sure to have that media officer in place so they can act to protect your campus, students, and staff.

With every media liaison officer put in place, just be sure that they are provided with the facts, and they can provide the media with the information they need for their story.

Also, the media liaison officer will be the face of your school, so they should be someone who comes across as being respectful to the situation that is happening.

Having all these steps in place is vital for your crisis plan to work when it comes to any deaths and handling bereavement, so that you know how to deal with it before any event actually occurs.

WRAPPING IT UP

We've now come to the end of this chapter which has touched on a few different topics.

First, we focused on SPED, including law and response interventions. Then, more generally, we considered student discipline. Finally, we looked at crisis plans, with an emphasis on handling death and bereavement.

If you're happy that you have understood all these topics well, move on to the next chapter, which takes a deep dive in to educational law.

16

EDUCATIONAL LAW

*W*e're now at the penultimate chapter of this part of the book that is designed to help you pass the multiple choice section of the SLLA 6990 with a high success rate.

In this chapter, there are many legal terms and definitions that you must comprehend, and you will need to know these as a leader. You will also need to know the legal concepts.

Hopefully, by the time you have digested the information contained in this chapter, as well as that from the other eleven chapters, you will have a strong basis to succeed in the multiple choice part of the test.

HOW MANY QUESTIONS ON THE TEST ASK ABOUT LAW?

Some SLLA 6990 tests may not have that many questions about laws, whereas others may be littered with laws. There is no real way of predicting it, and the number of law-related questions varies with every updated version.

Your best bet is to get caught up on all the laws you need to know in case any are asked about on the test. This will take longer than learning some of the other topics you need to know about on the test, but it is worth the added time.

You do not want to be in the position of kicking yourself because you are losing easy points and regretting not having brushed up on the laws.

It is a guessing game as to which ones will come up, so you are better off just learning all of them. As a leader, you will need to know these laws anyway, so it is better to learn them sooner rather than later.

Also, if you see "public interest" on the test, it means it deals with legal issues. If there is a question along the lines of, "how does *public interest* play into education," the answer is that public interest is anything dealing with laws that affect the general public's interest (civil rights, social justice issues, health, finances, well-being, poverty issues, etc.).

The first four specific laws are The Lau Decision, The Hazelwood Decision, The Weingarten Decision, and the Equal Access Act.

THE LAU DECISION

The Lau Decision states that you must have support for your English Learners (EL), English Language Learners (ELL), and English-as-a-Second Language (ESL) students.

Support must be provided for them, no matter how many students you have classified as EL on your campus. According to this law, even if you only have one EL/ESL/ELL student, you must have the resources and provide support for that student.

THE HAZELWOOD DECISION

For the Hazelwood Decision, let me tell you how it was reached. I will tell you the scenario and then what decision was made.

There was a school newspaper, and the school sponsor (the teacher sponsor) of that newspaper sent it to the principal and specified that they had approved it for publication.

The principal saw two articles deemed inappropriate to publish, such as one of them containing a student's name in it, which would have infringed on their privacy. So, the principal then sent the school newspaper back to the teacher sponsor, requesting that the two articles be edited.

The principal was not demanding that the articles be taken out of the newspaper, only that they were edited slightly, in one case to omit the name of a student so that the student would remain anonymous.

In response, the teacher sponsor replied that they did not have time to edit the two articles as they had to send the newspaper to print and publish as soon as possible because it was too close to the deadline.

Instead of editing the articles, the teacher chose to cut the two articles out of the newspaper before then sending it off to get printed and distributed.

The two students whose articles were cut sued the school on the grounds that they were being censored, and the school had no right to do so. They argued that the school could not just cut their articles out of the paper, and they had a right not to be censored.

The decision was that the school did, in fact, have a right to cut the articles. The school sponsored the paper; therefore, they had the right to edit it in any way that they wished.

Also, the school had the right to stop anything they felt would interfere with the learning process. So, if these articles would have caused more drama on campus, especially with certain students being named, the school absolutely had the right to stop it from being published.

The Hazelwood Decision is good to know because it demonstrates that leaders have certain responsibilities to protect students, particularly if something might take place which would interfere with the learning process.

THE WEINGARTEN DECISION

The Weingarten Decision says that any employee has the right to representation when being questioned by an employer in a situation that might lead to disciplinary action.

This means that if, for example, a teacher is about to be called into the principal's office to be reprimanded or even suspects they may be about to be reprimanded, fired, or anything else that the employee feels may lead to disciplinary action, then they can demand representation to accompany them in that meeting.

This applies to any employee and all staff and isn't limited to a teacher going into the principal's office, as with the above example.

The kinds of representation an employee may request could be their union representative, a professional organization representative, or anyone of their choosing that can accompany them to the meeting to represent them. Another example of a representative may be an employee's lawyer being present in the meeting.

The representative can join the meeting at any time, either at the beginning if the employee has requested in advance or if the meeting is already in progress and the employee decides that they would prefer their representation to be present. The employee can demand the meeting be paused or rescheduled until the representation arrives.

Through the Weingarten Decision, every employee has the right to representation in a situation that might lead to disciplinary action, whether that representation is present from the start or the employee opts to pause a meeting and ask for the representation.

THE EQUAL ACCESS ACT

The Equal Access Act says that a school must treat all student-initiated clubs equally if they fall into three categories: 1) The school is a public school, 2) It receives federal funds, and 3) The student club is a limited open forum.

Let's unpack this last point and understand what a limited open forum means. A limited open forum happens when a school allows one or more non-curriculum student groups to meet on campus during non-instructional time.

On the test, they might ask you questions about student clubs and when to allow certain student clubs. The question might appear as a scenario, and it essentially asks you if you should allow the club or not.

So, if a student comes to you and wants to initiate a club, you must treat them equally. A limited open forum is a student group that you allow that is non-curriculum-based that meets on campus. This would not be the math club, the science club, or another kind of curriculum-related club, but it would be a student club that is non-curriculum based and takes place on campus, but during non-instructional time.

Do notice here the verbiage and the law. It says equal, so if you decide to shut down all the clubs, then you have treated them all equally.

However, if you allow one of them to meet, then you must allow all of them to meet. If you give funding to one of the clubs, then you also must give all of them funding.

Whatever club you allow, be aware that you'd need to allow all kinds of clubs and can't discriminate one over the other.

TITLE LAWS

There are several Title Laws, and with time you could learn them all, but for now let's focus on Title I, II, III, and IX. These are the ones you most likely will be questioned on. If you at least know what these Title Laws are about, it can help you answer the questions that feature these laws.

Without knowing all the ins and outs of each law, you can gain an overview of what the law is about.

Title I relates to students in poverty situations or students who are disadvantaged. So, if you see a question about Title I, you'll be able to recognize that the question is about students who fit this category.

Title I is all about improving the academic achievement of your students who live in poverty, or disadvantageous situations.

What Title I part A says is that eligible students who attend private school can get Title I services from a public school. If a child is eligible and attend private school, they can be eligible for some Title I services from public schools.

Title II focuses on adults and hiring highly qualified teachers, administration, and principals. Some of your teachers are paid out of Title II, so some of their jobs may come out of Title II funding.

Professional development comes out of Title II. All professional growth opportunities can be paid out of Title II funding.

Let's focus on Title II Part A. Title II is about adults, and teacher and educational leader advancement, making sure schools have appropriately qualified teachers and administrators.

Educator professional development is often funded from these monies. So, the purpose of Title II Part A (sometimes written as just Title II A) is to make sure that this is happening, but in a specific way.

Title II Part A is all about increasing students' academic achievement by improving the quality of teachers and principals/leaders. The law focuses on teacher preparation, hiring, induction, professional development, and the retention of teachers. So, ensuring high-quality teachers are hired, trained, and continue to learn and stay.

Some of the program requirements are that your school gets good teachers through appropriate recruitment and hiring practices. Sometimes districts will actually hire somebody just to take care of recruitment. Anything like that can come out of Title II part A.

It also states that there is a need to support and grow new teachers effectively by induction strategy. This includes new teacher programs and programs for teachers who may be teaching a different subject than what they usually teach.

The point is to have those programs set up so that teachers can continuously learn and keep developing and sustaining teachers through retention practices, class size reduction, and effective and continual professional development. All of this is part of Title II Part A.

Title III is about your EL/ESL/ELL and immigrant students. All of your English proficiency, English learners, and immigrant students come under Title III. So, at least when you see Title III, you will know to think of EL/ESL/ELL and immigrant students.

Often when people think of Title IX, they think of athletics because usually, when we hear about it, it is because the school did not let a girl play on the football team or they're not treating the softball team the same as they're treating the baseball team. It is this kind of issue that is often associated with Title IX.

Title IX is actually about all gender inequality in all aspects of education, not just athletics. It includes pregnant and parenting students, sexual harassment, single-sex education, or anything dealing with gender in education. LGBTQIA+ students are protected under Title IX, but the extent of those protections is being fought in the legal system. Title IX states that educational programs must operate in a nondiscriminatory manner and cannot retaliate against a person who reports unlawful educational practices.

For this section, I have covered the Title Laws, with particular emphasis on Title I, II, III, and IX. I also went into greater detail about Title I Part A and Title II Part A. For clarity, Title IV covers 21st Century Schools, Title V covers Flexibility and Accountability, Title VI covers Indian, Native Hawaiian, and Alaska Native Education, Title VII covers Impact Aid, and Title VIII covers General Provisions.

In time, you would need to be fully aware of all of these laws, but for now, it would be best for you to focus on the Title Laws that I have highlighted above.

504 SERVICES

A child does not need to qualify for SPED services to qualify for 504. All 504 means is that a child needs an accommodation to gain equity. In other words, a child needs an accommodation to be equal to where all the other students are when learning.

It could be something as small as the student needing to be at the front of the room to help the student focus on the same level of another student. This could be due to the student having ADHD or something else requiring that student to be right in the center of the instruction. That student would need to have that attention without any distractions.

This is giving the student accommodations. It changes the environment, not the instruction and helps produce an equitable instructional/learning environment for the student.

You may see the acronym "FAPE," which stands for Free Appropriate Public Education. Under Section 504, FAPE states students who need accommodations must receive them to be equitable.

To be protected under 504, the student must:

1. Have a physical or mental impairment that actually limits one or more major life activities.
2. Have a record of that impairment.
3. Be regarded as having such an impairment.

Essentially, the physical or mental impairment must limit some part of their life, and then they could qualify for 504. Examples of accommodations include verbal testing, extended time, reduced questions/homework, preferential seating, and visual, verbal, or technological aids.

FERPA

The Family Educational Rights and Privacy Act (FERPA) is an important law. You should definitely know about FERPA for the SLLA 6990.

FERPA is to education what HIPAA is to healthcare. Essentially, it is a data privacy law that protects people's rights in the education system.

FERPA law states that a child's parents own the student record until the student reaches 18. It is determined by actual age and not what grade level the student has reached by that time. The student still can legally take ownership of the record when they become 18.

Until the student reaches 18, FERPA says that the parents are eligible to take ownership of the records.

Once 18 or older, the student themselves then has a right to inspect and review the student record. They also have the right to request that any corrections are done on the student record. The parent has this right until the student turns 18.

However, if the student is over 18, meaning they now legally control their record, but they are a dependent on their parent's income tax, the parent still has a right to those educational records and the legal control of the record remains the right of the parent.

With FERPA, you must seek the written permission of the owners to share a student's record with anyone apart from certain exceptions listed in the law.

School officials with legitimate educational interests may view the record, e.g., if the counselor needs to use that record, then it can be shared.

A police officer with a subpoena is another example, or if a student leaves your school and goes to a different school, you can send that record to the other school without written permission. These exceptions are covered in the FERPA law.

Appropriate officials may use these exceptions to the law in cases of health and safety emergencies. Do note the word "emergency." What if a health official asks to see the student's record, such as a student's psychiatrist asking to see the record in order to provide treatment? This is not considered to be an emergency.

In this case, you would need to get permission from the parent to share the record. It would have to be a health and safety emergency to qualify.

For anything else, permission needs to be granted by the student's parents until they turn 18 when they can give their own permission.

CIPA

The Children's Internet Protection Act (CIPA) is also likely to come up on this test.

CIPA was designed mainly to protect children from harmful or obscene content accessible on the internet.

Any school that is part of the E-Rate program, which helps schools pay for technology, must follow the rules of CIPA. One of the CIPA rules states that the school or district must have an Internet safety policy. This type of policy ensures that students are not getting inappropriate content on the internet through measures such as filtering.

CIPA is about safety and keeping students away from potentially harmful content on the Internet. It does not cover everything, such as copyright laws, but is particularly focused on keeping children who use the Internet safe.

OTHER LAWS

As well as the laws stated in the preceding part of this chapter, there are some others you should research as they may have a small chance of coming up in the SLLA 6990. These other laws include the following:

- Disability Discrimination (which includes 504 law)
- Sex Discrimination (which is included in Title IX)
- Race and National Origin Discrimination (which is part of the Civil Rights Act)
- Individuals with Disabilities Education Act (IDEA)

ROUND-UP OF EDUCATIONAL LAWS

Having gone through this chapter, hopefully, you will now have a much better idea about some of the laws you may be asked about on the SLLA 6990.

There are four specific decisions/laws (The Lau, Hazelwood, and Weingarten Decisions, and the Equal Access Act) that you should know about that relate to education.

Then, you should also learn about some other laws, but know how they apply in particular to education. This includes the Title Laws (especially Titles I, II, III, and IX), 504 Services, FERPA, and CIPA.

This chapter regarding education laws is dense, so it may take longer than usual to absorb all the information. If you need more time to digest the information, pause here and give yourself that extra time. Go back and reread what you need to, as your time investment will be worth it in the long run.

17

OTHER TOPICS AND PRACTICE QUESTIONS

*Y*ou have now reached the final chapter in Part Three of this book, which is about the multiple choice section of the SLLA 6990 test.

As a reminder, in Part III, so far we have covered:

- tips on passing the multiple choice section
- resolving conflicts
- observations and feedback
- formulating and monitoring long term goals
- cultural responsiveness and program implementation
- leadership styles
- data

- supporting teachers and rigor
- professional development
- SPED, discipline, crisis plans, handling deaths and bereavements
- educational law

Now in this final chapter, we are going to look at five practice questions, but first, this chapter begins by covering other topics that may come up on the test, but are not substantive enough to dedicate an entire chapter to.

Even though these additional topics may only appear in one or two questions on the test, they are still definitely worth learning.

- Safety
- Using Technology
- Human Resources
- Families and Communities
- Effectiveness of Programs
- Professional Influence

At the end of this chapter, there is also the "thinking activity" for you to try, as it is the final chapter in this part of the book. It will then be time for you to move on to Part Four, which is all about the constructed response part of the test.

After that, you will be ready to take the test!

OTHER TOPICS ON THE TEST

Safety

Let's start with safety. Here are four examples of safety questions that could appear on the test. Of course, you will not see these questions, but think about what the questions are trying to get you to consider about safety.

- **You have construction in your school and the students are complaining because the construction workers are being rude to them. At the same time, the construction workers are complaining because the students keep walking through the construction zone. What do you do?**

Anytime you get a question like that, the first thing you could think about is putting up a physical barrier. This will notify the students exactly where they are not allowed to go.

- **You have destruction on one side of your building. Everything on that side of the building has been destroyed – including the classrooms. Do you shut down the library, which is on the undamaged side of the school, to hold classes?**

The answer here is yes. What's interesting about that question is it has the phrase "shut down," which sounds really negative and makes you want to say no. However, learning is paramount, so the needs of a classroom space outweigh the need to keep the library open.

Learning comes first, no matter what, and what you are doing here is creating "an alternative use of space." On seeing this kind of question, you may come up with various thoughts that may render this answer impossible, such as the library probably already has classes scheduled, and therefore the library is already used for learning.

Remember that the point of a test is to get the answers right, although we can all appreciate that this may differ from a real-world scenario. For the example question, there was no information about the library already being used. You only use the words on the screen, and no need to speculate about anything else. Only go by the information that has been provided to you, either as part of the question or as part of the answer.

- **Parents are dropping off students too early before school and then picking them up too late in the afternoon. What do you do?**

The kinds of answers you will be presented with here will include things such as having a meeting to make sure everybody knows the appropriate time for drop-offs and pick-ups or sending home the schedule again as a reminder.

However, this will not be the answer you need to select. You are a community leader. When you are a campus-level leader or a district-level leader, you automatically become a community leader. You are not just the leader of whatever position you're in; you're considered a beacon in the community, as your school and/or district forms an integral part of that community. Fully embrace your new role as a leader in the community. See if that changes your perspective of what your answer to the above question should be. If the parents are dropping off students too early and picking them up too late, this means that your community has a problem, and it has now become your responsibility to try to solve that because you are a community leader.

Therefore, the answer you will be looking for to solve this problem is that you will go to your superintendent and ask whether they have any funding to help you pay teachers to come early and stay late.

Your community has a problem. You are there to solve the problem, and that is the mindset you need to be in for this test.

- **You have a brand-new school and school opens next week. You send out a letter telling parents that the school will open next week, but the library is still under construction. Your parents get together and send you a letter back stating that they demand that you delay the opening of school until all the construction is completed, which is to keep the students safe. How do you handle that situation?**

Many people make a mistake and start answering the question with solutions such as putting all the books on a cart and still making sure that students have access to the library resources. You may indeed be providing students access to the library resources, but telling this to the parents would do nothing to alleviate their safety concerns.

In this example, the parents wrote you a letter saying that they want to delay the opening of school because of the construction due to their safety concerns. In response, you are offering continual access to library resources.

So, how should you actually be replying to this concern?

First, you need to let the parents know that you will not be delaying the opening of school. You cannot do that because the school has a duty to provide instruction to the students.

Next, emphasize that your number one concern is to keep the students safe. This addresses the parents' concerns. You are going to keep the students safe by erecting barriers and keeping them away from the construction zone, so there is no risk to their safety.

In addition, you will go one step further and inform the parents of the timetable so that they can know when the construction will end, the barriers will be removed, and the library will become fully operational.

Finally, make sure that your answer includes an element that communicates what you are doing with the parents. They are the ones who raised their concern, so be sure to communicate with them as part of your response. Now, of course we are discussing multiple choice here, but if you get in the right mindset of how you would handle these situations, it will help you choose the right multiple choice answer on the test.

Using Technology

Let's now look at technology.

- **Why is it important for you, as a leader, to update a web page or website?**

Nonetheless, let's take the premise of the test in that it is just double-checking that we are aware of why we need to do certain things with IT and technology. The question that they are asking is why you would want to show your students and your parents that you have updated a website. The answer is to show that learning is an ongoing process. It is to show that learning does not stop when they leave school. There are things on the website to help them after the school day ends. Learning is ongoing, not only within the school building and school hours.

- **What kind of language do you use when you update a website?**

They want to know that you are not going to try to dazzle anyone with jargon. They want to know that you are making the information you are providing accessible to all and not being exclusive to any particular audience.

This will become important with the constructed response part of the test as well. Often, people working in education use too much jargon.

As educational leaders, we are also community leaders. We must be inclusive of parents and the general public. Websites are there to inform the public, so we cannot include any jargon on them as they may alienate some sections of our audience.

- **Why do you need to have an acceptable use policy in place?**

Even if you adopt the same acceptable use policy from your district, you need to make sure that one is applied. It is your responsibility to oversee that as a leader.

Examples of guidelines that need to be included in your acceptable use policy dictate whether people can play games on the computers and when; whether they can listen to music; whether they are allowed to download music; which websites are permissible; whether they can access YouTube; or whether they can watch movies.

Acceptable Use Policies only state what is and what isn't allowed when using devices (what are the acceptable uses). It does not go any deeper than that. So if you see something about an AUP listing CIPA laws or having anything to do with legalities, that is not correct. It simply states what can be done while using devices.

One thing you should note is that the only way to really track students' Internet and device usage is by giving your students individual passwords. If the usage policy states that students cannot download music, the only way to see if the student did, in fact, download the music by reviewing the usage of their account by looking up their individual password that tracks what they're doing.

If all the students have a generic log-in and password, there is no accurate detail proving any individual student broke the acceptable use policy. Therefore, tracking usage by individual students' passwords is a perfect way to monitor and enforce your acceptable use policy.

- **How can you effectively use your technology staff?**

It makes sense that whatever goals you have for those technology staff must actually meet the school's instructional goals. Therefore, the technology goals must match the school goals.

- **On your campus, what is your plan in place for the acquisition, maintenance, and refreshing of your technology?**

This means that it would be best if you had a plan for how to get technology, fix it, and replace it on your campus.

Human Resources and Financial Management

Here are the kinds of questions that you may get about human resources and financial management:

- **What is the biggest challenge in education?**

Attrition

- **What is attrition?**

The hiring and keeping of good people

- **Why is attrition the biggest challenge in education?**

Lack of administrative support

- **Where does funding originate?**

The bulk of your funding comes from local and state tax dollars. The rest comes from federal tax dollars.

There are "restricted" and "unrestricted" funds. Restricted money is limited to one area. So, for example, you may have a fund for purchasing textbooks, which is restricted to that. Because the money is restricted, this means that even if your buildings are falling apart, or you need to buy some more pencils, you cannot spend your textbook fund on that because it is restricted, and it must be spent on textbooks only.

Unrestricted funds can be used on anything for your campus. An example is your general fund. Now, let's discuss allocating funds.

- **You've been awarded a large grant; how will you allocate this money?**

Your response is you allocate the funds according to your student data and your student needs.

If your student data indicates that your student performance is low in science, then you're going to allocate some money to that subject. You may need to get some manipulatives; you may want to build a new science lab. Because science needs improving in your school, you are going to use your new funding to improve that area.

You do not need to worry about what the other departments think. Your role is to allocate the funds where it is needed most in the school at that time. It is not about equality; it is about equity. As we looked at in a previous chapter, it is about giving everyone what they need to get on the same level to become equal.

So, keep in mind that as a leader, you need to allocate funds according to student needs and student data.

- **If the school budget is cut, your teachers still need supplies to teach. What would you do as a school administrator?**

In this scenario, you are going to have to tell the teachers to get the supplies they need, and the school will reimburse them. We don't know where this magical funding will come from, but teachers must have supplies in order to fulfill the school's vision. They cannot successfully instruct without the supplies they need. Hopefully, you can see why this is the solution in this example, as it fits with the mission. Take a look back to earlier parts of this book, including the logistics section, if you need to remind yourselves why this is the case.

- **How do you deal with accepting gifts?**

First, speak with your supervisor – the superintendent. They will decide if you can accept the gift or not.

Second, you should determine whether or not the gift has an educational benefit. If a company wants to give you a Lamborghini, you cannot accept it – unless you're going to use that Lamborghini for auto mechanics lessons or driver training education. Then, you would be accepting the gift because it has an educational benefit to it.

Third, the educational gift the school or district accepts will not take away from the annual budget. So, if you get $5 per student and someone gifts your school or district with 1 million dollars, you still would get $5 per student.

- **You will likely be asked a question about the welfare of students.** Any time that you get a question like this, consider them to be your health questions. In other words, these are questions about your students' health, such as whether there are bodily fluids on the floor, there is mold on the ceiling, or there is asbestos, and your students are getting sick.

For any environmental safety and students' welfare question that you get, always choose the answer that shows the highest level of concern. If the highest level of concern means calling the president, then do that. If it means calling the health department, then do that. If it is calling every sick student to see how they are feeling, then go with that.

Go with the highest level of concern you can show, and that will be your answer.

Families and Communities

There is only really one type of question you will probably get asked on the test in this regard:

As mentioned before, as a school leader, you are a community leader. This means that the school itself is a community center, as your school belongs to the community.

If your community asks to use your school, first of all, you're going to be non-discriminatory. The school is open to everyone.

You are also allowed to let your school be used for other things. The only thing that you will have to make sure of is whether your insurance covers the activity. If your insurance covers the activity, then you are allowed to let it happen.

There may be additional factors you are questioning about this now, such as who will be there to open up the premises? Who will be there to close it? Who is going to tidy up? Just remember that, as with all other questions on this test, it is taking place in a perfect world.

These kinds of practical issues are swept to the side, and the only element you need to be aware of to get the question right is that you are allowed to let your school be used for different activities, so long as your insurance policy covers it.

Effectiveness of Programs

These should be the easiest questions on the test as there is only one answer to them.

You may be asked what is essentially the same question about the effectiveness of your programs in different ways.

However, no matter how the question is phrased, there is only one answer. I cannot stress this enough, the answer is student data. You must go by student data to measure the effectiveness of any program you put into place.

The only way you can tell if your lunch schedule is working, the only way you can tell if your professional development is working, and the only way you can tell if *anything* is working is by using student data to measure the effectiveness.

Professional Influence

There are two layers to your professional influence: advocacy and support.

- In the first influence, you are there as an advocate for your school. You should be there to fight for everything you need for your school.

Your school, your campus, or your district office is your baby. You need to fight. You need to go to the superintendent, go to the school board, and go wherever you need to go to advocate for your school, campus or district office. If not you, then who?

Now, the flip side of that is that you must support whatever decision is made (whether it be by your school board, your superintendent, or the legislature). This means that now you leave behind being an advocate and move to being supportive.

So, if you've been fighting for a new science lab, for example, and the whole community knows that you've been fighting for this new science lab, but in the end, the district says no to it, that's when you have to flip from advocacy to support, especially in front of your staff.

In front of your staff, you now must be supportive of that school board's decision. You can say to them, "Guys, we fought a good fight, but they had their reasons." No matter what, you must be supportive of that school board's decision.

So, to clarify, there are two levels of your professional influence — advocacy and support – and you must know when to adopt each role.

PRACTICE QUESTIONS

In this section, I will be giving you examples of questions and answers.

If you feel confident that you understand all the additional topics and all those that came before, you are ready to go through the next section.

I did not create all of these questions and found some of them through trainings, conversations and educator-created test prep materials on websites such as Quizlet. The explanation of the answers are my own.

Practice Question 1

An elementary school leader has received complaints about several students who have been engaging in name-calling and verbal harassment at their school bus stops. No physical violence has been reported. Which of the following actions would be more appropriate for the leader to take *first* in response to these complaints?

a. Assign the students to different buses and warn them and their parents/guardians that further complaints will result in being banned from riding the bus.

b. Refer the complaints to the school-based management team for immediate attention.

c. Meet with each of the students to state that their behaviors at the bus stop are unacceptable and inform their parents/guardians of the complaints.

d. Direct faculty members to visit the bus stops to observe the students and provide warnings as needed.

Practice Question 2

The leader of a high school is allocating funds to support the work of the school's newly established professional learning communities (PLCs). Which of the following expenditures will best support the growth of the PLCs?

a. Paying for the training of the teacher leaders who facilitate and oversee the work of the PLCs.

b. Purchasing a commercial program that focuses on inquiry-based learning.

c. Hiring a staff person to plan and monitor the work of the PLCs.

d. Compensating teachers for time spent meeting in their PLCs after school hours.

214 | DR. DESIREE ALEXANDER

Practice Question 3

The current placement system into English language classes at J.S. Clark High School is a norm-referenced test, but advancement to the next level of instruction is based on criterion-referenced tests. The high school's choice of criterion-referenced test is appropriate for advancement within its English language program because a criterion-referenced test can

a. Determine if students have attained a desired level of skills and abilities.

b. Be administered to a large group at one time.

c. Determine which students are performing better than their peers.

d. Identify a normal distribution of test scores.

Practice Question 4

To obtain community support for future projects and initiatives, a school leader wants to update community leaders and stakeholders about new academic programs and other recent achievements at the school. Which of the following actions is the most effective way for the school leader to accomplish the goal described?

a. Calling the local legislative representative to discuss recent school successes as well as necessary facility upgrades.

b. Sending parents a newsletter that highlights the achievements of high-performing students each semester.

c. Inviting parents and community members to provide feedback while attending seasonal events at the school.

d. Posting the school's achievements each month on the websites for the school and the district.

Practice Question 5

Of the following, the best way for a leader to encourage a person within a group to participate productively is to

    a. Provide adequate rewards for accomplishing a task.

    b. Increase congruence between individual and group goals towards the area of school improvement.

    c. Try to ensure that enough conflict is generated to maintain interest.

    d. Increase the number of acceptable ground rules for the group.

PRACTICE QUESTION ANSWERS

Practice Question 1

First of all, let's break down the anatomy of a question.

- "An elementary school leader has received complaints about several students who have been engaging in a game calling in verbal harassment at their school bus stops. No physical violence has been reported."

Which of the following actions would be more appropriate for the leader to take first in response to these complaints?"

The first thing you are going to get is what's called a *scenario*. As you can see, this is the first part of the question.

The scenario is where they are setting up what is happening in this question – in this space, in this world. You are being shown the snapshot of a scene – the *scenario*.

The funny thing is, sometimes, this scenario is vital for answering the question. At other times, you do not need a word of it to answer the question.

This is a good skill to learn when you are taking those practice tests. Start by asking yourself the question: "Do I need this scenario?" If you discover that you do need the scenario, then ask yourself what you need out of the scenario to be able to answer the question.

The second part is the actual question, and here it is again: "Which of the following actions will be most appropriate for the leader to take first in response to these complaints?"

The third part is the keyword in the question which changes the meaning of the question, *first*. When you see this, it means that many of the answers will be correct, but which one will you do FIRST.

The answer is C: Meet with each of the students to state that their behaviors at the bus stop are unacceptable and inform their parents/guardians of the complaints.

You can think about this one as due process. You are acting on the information because you were not there. You received these complaints, so you need to give due process to find out what actually has been happening.

Start by meeting with those students to have a discussion with them to let them know that complaints have been received, which means that something is not right about their behavior at the bus stop.

After you do that, you need to inform them that you're going to get their parents involved because they also need to know.

Then, even if you find out that nothing happened at the bus stop, you have still acted on a complaint.

Practice Question 2

- "The school leader of a high school is allocating funds to support the school's newly established professional learning community or PLC. Which of the following expenditures will best support the growth of the PLC?"

The answer is A: Paying for the training of the teacher leaders who facilitate and oversee the work of the PLCs.

You want to get away from answers that use external motivation versus internal motivation. If you have an answer that says you are going to give a teacher *something* to do *something*, then that's probably not going to be your answer. It should be that the teacher is doing *something* because the teacher feels it is right.

If the teacher does not feel it is right, then the onus is on you as a leader to show them that it is correct; show them what's right. You should not give them external motivation or reward as you would sometimes do with students. The answer should be that you are leading educators/adults to understanding that it should be done simply because it is the right thing to do.

In this case, you are not going to hire one person to only oversee PLCs, but you are going to pay for the training. Therefore, you are paying for the growth of the teacher leaders who are going to facilitate and oversee.

This is an important element as you are paying for them to grow. You are paying for them to train to facilitate and oversee the PLCs.

If an answer appears that says something like you purchase a commercial program that focuses on inquiry-based learning, you can consider this a "red-herring" answer and one that you can easily avoid. This issue of inquiry-based learning has popped up out of nowhere and is not in the question, so you can easily scratch that one off.

Practice Question 3

- "The current placement system into English language classes at J.S. Clark High School is a norm-referenced test, but advancement to the next level of instruction is based on criterion-referenced tests. The high school's choice of criterion-referenced test is appropriate for advancement within its English language program because a criterion-referenced test can..."

The answer is A: Determines if students have attained the desired level of skills and abilities. But, let's break down this question further to examine why that's our answer.

First, what do you need to know from this scenario? What is this question actually asking? If you break it down, all this question asks is what a criterion-referenced test is. So, all you need to know is what a criterion-referenced test does. You do not have to know about anything else, such as the English language program.

So, if you know what they are asking you, you can clearly see what the answer is, which, as stated above, is that criterion-referenced tests focus on content (do you know the content...did you learn the skills). You really did not have to know anything from the scenario to answer this question correctly.

Practice Question 4

- "To obtain community support for future projects and initiatives, a school leader wants to update community leaders and stakeholders about new academic programs and other recent achievements at the school. Which of the following actions is the most effective way for the school leader to accomplish the goal described?"

First of all, let's examine the question, which asks, "which of the following actions is the most effective way for the school leader to accomplish the goal?" Therefore, let's determine what the goal is.

The goal is to obtain community support for future projects and initiatives. How will he accomplish the goal? By updating community leaders and stakeholders about new academic programs and other recent achievements at the school.

Let's go through your answer choices before discussing the right answer. What may our thought processes be?

In answer A, we have one stakeholder in the local legislature representative. Good start. So we have a stakeholder to discuss recent school successes, but the answer mentions necessary facility upgrades, which is not mentioned in the question.

In answer B, we are sending parents a newsletter highlighting the achievements. Great! We have stakeholders in the parents and we are discussing the achievements at the school. However, we are only discussing the achievements of the high-performing students. That was not how we wanted to achieve our goal. We wanted to discuss new academic programs and achievements of the entire school, not just the high-performing students.

This answer looks better than the first one. Still probably not right, but between the two, you have now just ruled out the first option. You will stick with sending parents a newsletter as the potential answer until a better one comes along.

In answer C, we are inviting parents and community members to provide feedback while attending seasonal events. We have multiple stakeholders (parents and community members). YAY! Finally! However, while this starts to look like the best answer, it is actually the worst answer of the four.

The action to achieve our goal is to update community leaders about new academic programs. This answer is saying that you want to get feedback. The action in the scenario is I want to give them information, but this answer says that I want to get information from them. This cannot be right as the answer doesn't match the question at all. This answer is actually in direct opposition of the scenario. In this instance, I am still going to go back to answer B as being my best answer.

But the answer is D: Posting the school's achievements each month on the websites for the school and the district. This means information is being shared with a larger number of stakeholders because if they're a legislator, they may not go to the school website, but they would go to the district's website to learn more about the district that they're involved with.

As a higher-level stakeholder, they may not be involved in that individual school, but they will be involved with the district. So that is going to mean even more stakeholders. As you are trying to reach the most stakeholders, this one is your answer: to post on the school and district websites.

This answer is the only answer that does what the question asks you to do.

Practice Question 5

- "Of the following, the best way for a leader to encourage a person within a group to participate productively is to…"

The answer is B: Increase congruence between the individual and the group goals towards the area of school improvement. In other words, the way to get a person to participate is to show them you share the same goals. You can show them that everyone is on the same page and on the same track.

Remember that offering external rewards to adults is not the answer. You want internal rewards versus external rewards. And even though conflict is not negative, you should never try to cause it for the sake of entertainment. And lastly, *increase ground rules* is a negative answer and a management answer (not a leader answer).

Coming across as autocratic may suggest that you are a participant in the group but not committed, and this doesn't solve your problem. The only answer that shows congruence is ensuring that the person in the group that you want to engage understands that the whole group's goal matches with their individual goal. You need them to participate in this teamwork to help students excel. They are more likely going to participate when everyone gets on the same page and they see a benefit from participating.

I have had MANY people tell me they got this last question wrong because they were not quite sure what congruence meant. One final tip is as you are taking practice tests and studying, you will come across words and concepts you do not understand. LOOK IT UP! This is your study time, so anything that you do not understand or anything that you want to know more about, this is the time to research it. Something on the test is going to punch you in the gut because you do not know what it means. It happens to all of us. But, if we get that gut-punch during your practice, you are lucky because you get to research it. Don't be prideful! If you don't know something, who cares? That is why you are studying! Research it now so you will be ready for the real test!

SUMMARY

You have reached the end of the multiple choice section of our SLLA Test Prep.

Hopefully, those five practice questions above have given you a really good idea of what mindset you need to be in when answering questions and how to break down the questions and answers to choose the correct one.

In the next part of this book, there are chapters dedicated passing the constructed response part of the test. Before moving on, please try the thinking activity below, which will help you contextualize all that has been covered in part three of this book.

THINKING ACTIVITY

Many topics are covered in this section. Some you may feel comfortable with, while some you need more time to explore.

This is that time! Make a list of the topics and vocabulary to explore and start researching.

You can find some resources here: www.educatoralexander.com/slla-test-prep

PART IV

CONSTRUCTED RESPONSE

18

TIPS FOR PASSING CONSTRUCTED RESPONSE

*Y*ou have now reached Part Four and the final part of this book. This part of the book is designed to provide you with information on how to pass the constructed response section.

You will get 1 hour and 15 minutes to answer the four equally weighted questions in the constructed response section, meaning that you want to spend around 18 minutes per question.

NO NEED FOR ESSAYS

For the constructed response part of the test, they are not looking for essays as answers. They are also not looking for grammar or complete sentences (however, you will have complete sentences if you follow my tips). They are not testing to see how eloquently you can write. They want to see whether you actually know the information they are seeking. They want to know if you know how to handle the situation presented to you. The whole point of this test is to determine whether you are ready to be an entry-level administrator.

With this in mind, you can now start thinking about the kind of technique you're going to adopt to provide answers with maximum impact in a relatively short period of time – just 18 minutes per question.

USE BULLET POINTS OR PARAGRAPHS

You can actually use bullets or paragraphs on the constructed response part of the test. I usually tell people to write the opposite of what they're used to writing. So, if you are a frequent writer, you are the kind of person that is used to writing in paragraphs. In this case, write in bullets, as this will make you get to the point faster.

On the other hand, if you are a person who doesn't like to write, then I would encourage you to write in paragraphs because then you are forcing yourself to think it all through and spell it out more. You are forcing yourself to write more, and more likely to get across the points and not miss anything.

You need to make sure that your answers for the constructed response section are succinct and to the point. There is no room for extra "fluff." You do not have enough time to write things that have nothing to do with answering the question.

KEEP TO THE POINT

Do not try to impress the examiners who are scoring your constructed response. There is no need for any superfluous information, such as your educational background or anything you are proud of, which you feel would add weight. Just get to the point, and the examiners will appreciate that.

They want to know whether you know how to handle the situation. It will not add any value or impress the examiners if you start sprinkling in information about your educational attainment or things you've learned. Leave any of that fluff stuff out of your answers. Be very plain and clear in your answer. In summary, stick to the point, answer the question, explain your answers well, and use plain language in your answer!

HOW THE GRADING WORKS

Each question in the constructed response is worth 1 to 3 points, or 0. Your constructed response answers get sent to two different examiners across the United States for grading. For example, it could go to somebody in Louisiana and someone in New Jersey; then they grade it.

If there is some discrepancy between the two grades you received from the examiners in Louisiana and New Jersey – let's say you get a 3 from the first examiner but a 1 from the other examiner – then your answer is sent to a third person.

However, if your score from the original two examiners matches, then that is the score that goes forward.

Here are some other things to know about this process. First, the test is anonymous, so they will not know who you are. They will not have your name, and they will not know where you are from.

Second, they will not grade the whole test. Each examiner is only sent individual questions to be graded.

Examiners are sent individual questions and answers, so what they see when they are grading is the question, plus some guidance on how to grade it (points that should be included in the answer). Using these guidelines, they score your answer. How do I know this information? Because I once served as a grader for ETS.

Because of this, when you are writing out your answer, do not refer to other answers. So, do not write things like, "as I wrote in the previous answer, I am going to form that same committee." This will not make sense to the examiners, and they will not know what you're talking about as they only see individual questions, not anything else you've written. Each question is a completely fresh answer. Think of it as starting a completely different test on each question.

The third thing is that this means you can repeat yourself in different answers. In fact, in some cases, you may need to. So, if you find yourself having to repeat yourself in the answers, and that feels unnatural, do not worry, as it's perfectly normal, and you'll probably need to repeat yourself on the test.

For example, if forming a committee makes sense as part of your first answer, then don't be afraid to make the same response for another question. If something is best practice, you will probably use it in more than one answer, like forming a committee. So, it is acceptable to repeat yourself.

The fourth thing you should know is that there is no need to quote the scenario or the data that much. They can see what is in the question, and you can just get on with answering it. So, bear this in mind as a tip to not waste time.

You can quote a bit of what is in the scenario if you want to; it is not as if they will mark you down for it, but you don't have to. It is not the conventional kind of technique where you are supposed to pull things down into an essay as part of the answer because your answers need not be written in essay format.

SUMMARY OF TECHNIQUE

You want to show the examiners exactly how you will handle the situation so that they know that you know your stuff. To simplify this, you can get straight to the point and write your answer as bullets or write your answers in paragraphs depending on your writing style. Make sure everything you want to say is included in plain language. Make it easy for them to grade. You can look at it as a job interview. You want to leave all of your great ideas on the page. No one will ask you what you mean by what you wrote, so make sure it makes sense and it is all written out. Keep it specific and explain each answer you include (we will discuss this more later).

It is very important that you keep your answers succinct and straight to the point to deliver a direct message and not unnecessarily waste time. Get into this mindset, and adopt this approach, and you are likely to get a score of 3 points (the maximum) for each of your answers in the constructed response part of the test.

Next up, we will be looking at how to deal with data in the constructed response part of the test, but first please make sure you have understood everything in this chapter, as knowing these techniques will thoroughly help you pass the constructed response part of the test.

19

HOW TO DEAL WITH DATA

*A*fter reading about general tips and techniques on how to pass the constructed response section, I'm going to spend the rest of this part of the book delving deeper into how you should answer the constructed response questions.

Next up is data, and you will see that there is a fair amount to cover in this chapter. Data will come up a lot in the scenarios that they provide you in the questions, so there are many different ways you will need to approach it.

However, my main advice is not to panic – follow the tips provided throughout this chapter, and you'll be sure to deal with data effectively in your constructed responses.

DIFFERENT TYPES OF DATA

In the questions of the constructed response part of the test, they may provide data to you in multiple ways.

For example, they may provide you with student test scores, a parent letter, a school improvement plan, etc. The test usually provides more data than you actually need to answer the question. Please read the question first and decipher which parts of the data are relevant to your answer.

It is not that the examiners are trying to trick you. They are attempting to simulate a real-life situation. Often in your role as an educational leader, you will be presented with actual scenarios that contain an abundance of data, and part of your job is to pick apart what is relevant and know what is important to handle the situation.

Just as it might happen in real life, on the test, you may be presented with five pieces of data, and then you are asked about one of those, but without any hint, because part of the skill is to know which data you will need.

So, keep this tip in mind. Do not just start going through all the data and making yourself sick with numbers and wasting time when you could have decided on your answer and already have started writing it out.

Some of the questions will ask you for a certain number of answers. Such as, some of the questions might ask something like, "give us two ways you can solve this." Some questions do not ask for anything specific, but they might ask something more general, such as, "how do you solve this?"

As a tip, if they do not ask you for a specific number of answers, put down three. If it is one of those questions that has an open question, such as, "how do you solve this," then provide three answers. Answers can be written as bullets, or if you prefer writing a paragraph, make sure it has three answers.

NEVER LEAVE YOUR ANSWERS UNFINISHED

One huge reason why many people fail this test is because they do not finish the constructed responses. You need to finish every question in the constructed response part of the test. Much of this comes down to exam technique and making sure that you are answering the questions so that you will not run out of time.

I have a couple of tips for you that you can do to make sure that you at least answer every question. Certainly, what you do not want to do is write a brilliant answer for one question, but then totally neglect all the other answers. It is much more sensible to answer all four constructed response questions, as it vastly increases your chance of success in the entire test.

In order to make sure you stick to the time limits, first, put the number of answers you need for the question and move on. So, if the question is asking you for two answers, think of your answers, put them down, and move on. If it does not ask you for any specific number of answers, write three answers and move on as per my tip above.

Be careful with this point and stick to three answers if it is an open-ended question. If you are thinking of more than three, that is great! However, focusing on one question for too long may hinder you from completing all four questions. So, put your best three answers and move on. Remember, you have just 18 minutes per answer, so you want to make sure that you have time to answer them all.

However, if you have answered all four questions but still have time left, you can go back to your previous answer and add some more information.

Now, here is my second tip, which *can* be applied by all test takers, but if you have **test anxiety,** then I do not suggest this tip for you.

Read over all of the questions, and start on your easiest question first. This not only lets you answer that question a little bit quicker so as to get it out the way, but getting your first answer done makes all the difference to build your confidence.

Even though you are diving in and writing your first answer according to what you considered to be the easiest, the fact that you read all four questions first means that you are also calculating those other questions in the back of your mind while you are writing your first answer.

You may not realize that you are thinking about it, but subconsciously you will be quietly thinking about your other answers. In the back of your mind, you will start thinking of those answers, and effectively what you have done is allow yourself more time.

However, this approach could overwhelm you if you have test anxiety. It could be way too much information at the same time making it harder to process. So, if you are likely to get test anxiety, I don't suggest you try this method.

TEST ANXIETY

Do be aware that test anxiety is a real thing. When you hear people talking about how their brain freezes or how they experience hot flashes when they take tests, they are probably suffering from test anxiety.

If you think you have test anxiety, definitely look into it. Do some research, look at what advice is available, and you may find some methods and tips that work better for you on how to pass the test. You can also look into how to apply for the test accommodations available on the ETS website.

KEEP YOUR BULLETS SPECIFIC AND AVOID JARGON

When it comes to writing your bullets, keep it to one step or answer per bullet. Within that answer, however, you should have the specific answer to the question and WHY that answer is important or HOW you came up with that answer. We will talk more about this later, but for every answer you give, you must have a WHY or a HOW.

Whether you use bullets or paragraphs, do not use jargon; use plain language. This is extremely important. As you know, this test is taken in about half of the United States, and your examiner could be from any of these states. (Remember, your answer is provided to two different examiners.)

Therefore, this means that some of the jargon you use at your school, in your district, or in your state may not be known by everyone, including the examiners. So, avoid jargon at all costs.

Another problem is that some of the words, abbreviations, and acronyms actually mean something different somewhere else. So, using any jargon (PLC, RTI, PGP, etc.) in this sense is also a no-go.

For example, I started my teaching career in Louisiana, and we did something called a professional growth plan. The professional growth plan there is where we put down the ways that we wanted to grow professionally that year. For example, you would state that you wanted to go to a certain conference, or you wanted to attend a workshop, or you wanted to learn about something somewhere, or gain a skill in something else.

This document was completed and submitted at the beginning of the year, so I did that when I was there in Louisiana. Then, I moved to Texas and started teaching. When I got there, I asked when we needed to complete our professional growth plan for the Dallas area. Goodness me, people looked at me as if I were crazy! I did not understand what was wrong, but then eventually, I got to the bottom of it.

For them, a professional growth plan is used in a situation where your principal would document how you are not doing what you are supposed to do, or you are not effective as a teacher, and this is why you are forced on a professional growth plan that tells you how you need to grow and improve.

For them, a professional growth plan was seen as a reprimand, which is why they were shocked that a teacher was asking for one voluntarily!

Thus, you can see how all jargon can have a different meaning depending on where you are and can easily be misunderstood. Never assume that what you understand something to be is the same as what others understand of it.

Let's say I was doing the test. As part of my answer, I wrote something about what I'm going to do with a new teacher: provide them with a professional growth plan. If someone from Texas were grading it, they would think I were reprimanding my new teacher (remember that reprimanding new teachers is a big "no").

In fact, you were giving them a professional growth plan to help them, but the examiner thinks you were doing it for the opposite reason. So, this stands as an example of exactly why you must be very careful about using any jargon on the test.

Also, always think twice about using any terminology that is not completely clear. Never assume that everyone will know what your terms mean or how they are applied.

You would not want to fail a question just because your terminology was lost in translation. To make sure you are not using any jargon, imagine that you are writing to a parent – you are communicating with an interested party, but a non-specialist.

Do not use technical jargon that may cause any confusion. So, for example, instead of saying something like, "I'm going to bring up test scores by using Accelerated Reader," consider that not everybody knows what Accelerated Reader is. It is essentially a piece of jargon.

Even though it is a national reading program, the examiner may not specialize in the particular subject, so they may not know what it is. They certainly will not look it up to grade your paper either, so you would lose points simply because you used a term that you assumed everyone would know the meaning of, but they do not.

Always explain everything plainly and avoid jargon or terms that could have double-meaning or cause confusion.

Examiners know what to look for in the answers. They are testing whether people are ready to become educational leaders, but this does not mean they will have a particular specialism in any subject.

So, even if you are an English teacher and know what the Accelerated Reader is, you should not assume that anyone else will or should know. Instead, you need to describe what you are talking about.

Explain how it works. Explain that you are going to use a reading program that uses student reading levels to help students pick their books. That way, you have avoided the assumption that people will know the jargon.

Write your answers as if you are writing for someone who is not in education. Another way of putting it is to "keep it simple," but not in a bad sense. All you're trying to do is appeal to the widest audience.

Do not use jargon. Just assume no one knows the definitions of the words you are using, so explain and describe what you are talking about instead of using education jargon.

THIS TEST IS NOT THEORY

As a reminder, your test is practical, not theory. What the examiners are looking for is if you know how to handle the situation in the question.

For example, they want to know whether if you got promoted, and then something like the scenario happened to you on your first day as an assistant principal, would you instantly know the steps to take to resolve the issue? That is what they care about, and that is what the examiners are looking for – the practical steps. They are looking for you to demonstrate practice, not theory.

In the logistics section of this book, I mentioned that you have to imagine you are in a perfect world when taking this test. Your steps need to be positive with positive language. You are still in this perfect world at all times, but you need to identify very practical steps.

Again, you are not trying to save the world, and you are not trying to save all of education. All you are doing is demonstrating that you can handle this one single situation. So, in your answer, demonstrate your ability clearly, and show the examiners your steps/answers.

Think of it almost like each of your answers is a sub plan. This means that an examiner should be able to pick up your answer at any point and be able to understand it without asking any questions.

You can make sure of this by writing very specifically, telling the examiners why you are doing each step or how you found each answer. Also, for every answer you put, you have to say why it is important.

If you are writing your answer as bullets, then you need to tell the examiner why that step is important or how you found that answer in every single bullet. This is fundamental to passing the constructed response section: make your point specific and be explicit about why it's important or how you found it.

For example, if the question asks you for three steps to solve a problem, you should have two sentence starters to answer EACH step: *This is my first step* and *This step is important because...* If the question asks you for information, you should have two sentence starters to answer for EACH: *This is the information...that I found because...*(referring to the data) and *This information is important because...* We will discuss this process more later, but THIS is the formula to passing the constructed response part of this test.

BE SPECIFIC

As mentioned above, any part of your answer should be self-explanatory, meaning that the examiner is able to follow it without needing to ask any questions.

So, if part of your answer is that you're going to form a committee, don't leave your examiner needing to ask, "Who is on the committee?" "What will the committee do?" "Why is it important to form the committee?" Make sure these details are included in your answer.

As another example, if you have an answer that states that the data will need to be looked at, do not leave the examiners asking: "What data?" "Who's looking at it?" "Why is this important?" Always be explicit, and make it clear to the examiner why something you are doing is important and necessary. Be specific in your answers so that it does not leave any questions for the examiner.

In your answers, do not be generic. If you are too generic, the examiner won't know that you fully know the answer to the question, and they won't be sure to award you points. So, using the above example of forming a committee, you would need to go further and tell the examiners some specifics – such as your committee would consist of parents, students, and math teachers with the purpose of looking at math test data.

Here, you can see how this covers the "who" and "what" factors. You could also state that doing it this way is important because it is the best way to solve whatever the problem is in the question.

If you put it this way, that is a much better answer. So, please remember that you need to be specific in your answers. You also must state why you're doing something. Even if the reason seems obvious, you must assume whoever is reading it will not know. The examiner will only award points if the reasons are explicit, so don't forget to point this out with every step. And you can only be specific if you are connecting your question directly to the question at hand!

Here is another example: The question on the test asks how you bring up the reading scores. An answer that somebody types is that they are going to have a classroom library. Now, throw into the mix that if students have literature close to them, this means that they actually want to read and that they choose to read.

When the teacher gives students reading time, they are more likely to read something they really want to read. Also, it's in close proximity to them. Therefore, the more they actually read, the better their reading comprehension becomes, and the more vocabulary they acquire. The better their reading comprehension becomes will help them in all content levels. You can see here how providing a comprehensive "why" is important as part of your answer.

Provide the reasons in a similar way for every answer you give, and you will make it easy for the examiner to grade and give you full points!

You only get one shot at giving your answer, as nobody is going to come back and ask you for clarification. So, before you close off your answer, ask yourself "why?" first. If your

248 | DR. DESIREE ALEXANDER

answer does not fully explain everything – it is not self-explanatory – then make sure you are adding the necessary details.

DON'T FIGHT THE QUESTION

My last tip is not to fight the question.

I already mentioned this in the tips for answering the multiple choice section, and here it is again for the constructed response section. There is no point in fighting the question! All you have is the black and white on the screen. So, whatever they give you is what you have to work with.

Do not start tricking yourself by reading into what is not there. For example, if it was a similar question to the examples above, do not start thinking, "What if they will give me the math scores?"

They did not give you the math scores in the question they gave you. So, work with what you have. Move on and answer the question. To do anything more would be a waste of time, and time is in short supply during the test. Doubting yourself or the information in the question will not help you formulate an answer either. You must work with what you have got.

You know what they have provided, and this also means that it is what they want to provide you, and they have not made a mistake. They did not forget anything; they gave you exactly what they wanted to give you. Therefore, however the question appears, you have to answer it as it is.

I have mentioned this before, but there is a big emphasis on the test imitating real-life scenarios. As an educational leader, you will not always have everything you need to solve a problem. Yet, you are still going to have to solve the problem. This is very much how the questions are posed to you on the test, and they are also expecting you to be able to answer, even with limited information.

This also means that you should not bring anything additional into your answer. You should only formulate your answer from what is in front of you, not from additional sources. If they did not mention it in the question, do not bring it into the answer. You only have the information that is in black and white...don't assume anything more!

If you are doing any of these things, then you are fighting the question. Stop it – it will not help you!

Also, don't bring any "what ifs" into your answer. This will not help you to effectively provide the solution and will not pick up any points. I have seen some answers such as, "If he had started earlier, he wouldn't be in this problem."

This kind of answer will not help you. What you are presented within the question is what you have to work with. He is *already* in the problem, and it is not asking you what you would do if you had a crystal ball.

The question is showing you that he's already stuck and asking you what he should do now, not what he could've done if things were different – so avoid any "what ifs."

REMEMBER YOUR LIMITS AND USING DATA

Next, we are going to look at a data set, and I will be giving tips on how to read sets of data.

Usually, you will get a data set meant to be for the school and district you are working with. If they give you both data sets, this is for you to compare if you need to, or if they are only asking you about the school, you only have to answer about the school.

A good tip here is that if you get stuck, like if you cannot find something in the data, start comparing the school to the district IF you have district data. That is why the extra information is given to you. If you do not have this extra information, you then know that the answer is in the data you have already been given.

For example, let's say that the question asks you to look at the data (see table) and then list three good things, three bad things, or a combination of both. Do not get stuck on whether you must do three bad things or three good things. If they say this, then it means you could do three bad, three good, or a mixture of both.

Grade Five Test Results
Spring
School Summary

SUMMARY SCORES	VOC	RDG CMP	LNG MEC	LNG EXP	MTH CMP	MTH C&A	RDG TOT	LNG TOT	MTH TOT	TOT BTR
MEAN SCORES										
NUMBER RIGHT	28	28	19	37	34	30	53	56	60	169
SCALE SCORE	705	693	688	716	705	695	692	702	688	694
GRADE EQUIV	5.4	4.5	4.2	5.1	5.2	4.6	4.7	4.7	4.5	4.6
NATIONAL %ILE	78	63	57	64	73	63	67	61	68	67
NORMAL CURVE	66	57	54	57	72	57	59	56	60	59
% OF OBJ MAST	60	55	50	63	75	41				
STUDENT COUNT	43	43	43	43	43	43	43	43	43	43
NAT'L QTR %										
76-99	54%	32%	32%	30%	51%	28%	39%	25%	40%	37%
51-75	22%	21%	21%	33%	36%	35%	21%	30%	23%	23%
26-50	19%	35%	35%	33%	14%	21%	29%	40%	35%	35%
1-25	5%	12%	12%	4%	5%	16%	11%	5%	2%	5%

Legend

VOC	- Vocabulary	MTH C&A	- Math Concepts and Applications
RDG CMP	- Reading Comprehension	RDG TOT	- Reading Total
LNG MEC	- Language Mechanics	LNG TOT	- Language Total
LNG EXP	- Language Expression	MTH TOT	- Math Total
MTH CMP	- Math Computation	TOT BTR	- Total Battery

If you were given this data set, the first thing you would read is the title. This is important because it is where you get information that you need to answer the question. You will know that you're dealing with Grade Five and spring testing.

Grade equivalency is something that was mentioned in the multiple choice part of this book. This would mean that no matter whether it is spring testing, or starting in August or September, for Grade Five, you know that your grade equivalency will be 5.7 or 5.8. Usually, spring testing is about two months before the school year ends. This means that for grade five spring testing, grade equivalencies should be at a 5.7- 5.8.

The second thing you want to look at with the data is the legend at the bottom. Many people rush when they get the data and go straight to the middle. The top has some crucial information, so next would be to look at the bottom and take a look at what's there before reviewing the middle section of the data.

You do not have to read every single word in the legend, but it at least gives you a good idea of what you're looking at. This means that when you go to the middle of the data and start seeing some abbreviations, you will have an idea of what they refer to because you've already reviewed the legend. You can always go back to look at the legend again, but it is always a good idea to review it initially before examining the rest of the data.

GOING DEEPER INTO THE DATA

By now, you have looked at the top and bottom areas of your data, and therefore it is time to start examining the middle section. There is no need to feel nervous or intimidated by it; just know what to look for.

So, that would be my first tip in this regard: look for what you already know. This is not the time to try to start learning new skills. Use what you already know and move on. This is a test, and the point is to score as many points as possible.

Maybe after you finish the test, you could think about what was lacking and learn some new skills, but during the test is not the time to start trying to figure new things out.

So, let's take the above example and assume you are comfortable with looking at grade equivalency because you learned what grade equivalency was in the multiple choice section.

You can either look at the individual content areas, like vocabulary or comprehension or at the totals, but you wouldn't look at both.

So, for our example, we will look at individual content areas' grade equivalencies. For those we have 5.4, 4.5, 4.2, 5.1, 5.2, and 4.6. We already learned from the title that they should be in their fifth grade year during spring testing, and that should mean they are at a 5.7-5.8 grade equivalency. So, you're seeing that the grade equivalencies are low in every content area.

They are not on grade level in any area. Because remember, 5.4 tells me that they are in the fifth grade in the fourth month, when they should be in the seventh or the eighth month. So, considering the data, many of my students are still at the fourth-grade level.

That is the first thing that I would point out. Number one: the grade equivalency data shows me that my students as a collective are not on grade level. According to the title, they should be a 5.7-5.8 during spring testing since they are in grade five. I am going to include all that in my answer, and this would indicate that I can read the data.

So I have read the data and written my conclusion, but I missed something. I did not answer the question! It asked me to point out negatives or positives. I told them information, but did not answer if it was a negative or positive and WHY it is a negative or positive. Therefore, I would add this to my answer: *This is a negative because it means that my students will be leaving fifth grade soon and still be a the fourth grade or lower fifth grade level in many content areas.* Notice with these two answers combined I answered the question, I gave my why, I supported with data and I told how I concluded this from the data. This is a strong answer. The mistake many make is simply saying this is my conclusion from the data and it is negative. They do not say HOW they got to their conclusion from the data (because the title says they should be at 5.7-5.8) and do not say WHY this is a negative (because they will not be on grade level when they enter the next grade). This is how you pass this part of the test!

The whole point of this type of question is to prove that you can read the data. So, you need to demonstrate this to test scorers. Remember, you need to make your answers self-explanatory. Do not just say that as a collective, none of them are on grade level.

In your answer, tell them *HOW* you know that. Tell them you understand because of how you are reading the data.

Now that you have written your first point, you need to find something else on the data chart that makes sense to you (something that you already know about). You could try National Percentile. You know that percentile is whenever you see the number, it means that everyone else is below that number (this was covered earlier in this book).

For example, you can see that 78% of the nation is below your students in vocabulary, 63% of students in the United States are below your students in reading comprehension, and 57% of students in the United States are below where your students are in English mechanics.

Determining whether any of this is good or bad depends on how you write it up. You could say that your students are above 50% of the nation in all content areas, adding on that in vocabulary and math computation, they are over 70% of the United States students. So, this is a positive thing, even though the grade equivalencies are not where they need to be.

You could say that even though the national percentile shows that all of your students are over half of the United States, that is disappointing because your students are so low in their grade equivalency. The fact that your fifth grade students are on a fourth grade level, BUT they are over 50% of the US students in the same grade can be seen as a positive for your students, but a negative for the nation. Since the question did not ask you about the nation, you do not HAVE to put that, but it is a nice revelation that proves you know how to truly read the data and compare BOTH the national percentile with the grade equivalency with each other.

GIVING POSITIVE OR NEGATIVE REASONS

You now have your second answer, which is stating whether your findings are positive or negative, or a mixture of both. The third thing you can point out here is looking at objectives mastered.

You can figure out what that means. Objectives mastered means that it is the percentage of the objectives that your students actually mastered. So, the data says 16, 55, 50, 63, 75, and 41. Again, just like with the National Percentile, you must state whether this is good or bad, and you also need to say why.

Does it mean that it is good that your students have mastered 60% or 55%? Well, this is the end of the year, so you cannot say this is good. Your students have only mastered right around half, except for math computation, and that means right around half of the objectives.

However, knowing that their grade equivalencies are so low, it makes sense that they have only mastered that amount. So, in your answer, you can tell them it is bad, but also connect it to other data. This is a great technique to answer data questions such as these.

However, it makes sense that because there are still a lot left at the fourth-grade level, they can only master a certain number of objectives. So now, your third answer is down, and you can move on (remember, stick to threes).

Notice that I focused on the three things in the data: grade equivalency, national percentile, and percent of objectives mastered. So, this is sticking to three. However, you may want to point out something else. If they do this on your data sheet on your test, you may recognize it.

You may want to look at vocabulary and reading comprehension. Notice that the vocabulary is at a 5.4, but the reading comprehension is at a 4.5. So, essentially this means that they understand the words when they are in isolation, but they do not understand the words when they're in a sentence.

Something is off about that. They know what "different" means, but when I say, "two different men sang a song," they do not understand what different means anymore.

That tells me they are just memorizing the definition. They are not learning it because we know memorizing and learning are two separate things.

The students are memorizing it but not learning the meaning. Vocabulary is only being taught in isolation, which we know is a big "no-no." Essentially, this could mean that the students are just being taught a list of words for the week every night and not going any deeper with those words.

If you see something like this, then it's something you can point out in your answer. You can also see this with math computation and math concepts and applications. A similar thing could be that the data implies that the students know what 1+1 means, but when you try to get them to apply that, they don't know what you're talking about.

So, they know that $1+1 = 2$, but when you say, "Johnny has one apple and Bobby has one apple, how many apples do they have together," the students are confused. Something is not right about that. That means they are just memorizing a data table or something like that. They do not know how to apply it, which misses the point.

Further, notice the same thing happens in reading and math. So, was that put on the test for you to catch it? Look out for it. If you are not a math person, then you may not catch it in math, but you might catch it in reading. Take notice if they did it in both for you to try to catch it.

First, write your main answers out, and then if you have time, you can come back and put that extra piece of information as the fourth thing you've noticed about the data.

2ND DATA SET

There is also a second type of data set that you may encounter on the test. This data set will have you reviewing multiple-year data. This means you will be comparing data from more than one school year or test session. Any time you have multiple year data, you can look at it in two separate ways: year group or class.

This means you could compare, for example, 9th grade to 9th grade, 10th grade to 10th grade, 11th to 11th, and 12th to 12th – you are comparing by year group. For example, you can compare 2010's 9th graders to 2011's 9th graders. What happen in 2010 compared to what happened in 2011? Did students test scores increase, decrease, or stay the same? Then we can start analyzing the reasons behind the scores fluctuation so we can either try to do what we did again or change our practices. Or you could review it by the class.

So, you could look at the 9th-grade students who are now the 10th-grade students – comparing 9th to 10th grades. Looking at it this way, the 10th-grade students are now the 11th-grade students, and so on. You are comparing the class of 2025 to itself as the class continues through its grade levels. For example, you may want to ask why the class of 2025 did so well in science in 2019, but their scores fell over 50% in 2020. Then we can start analyzing the reasons behind it to decide to where to go with our teaching practices.

To clarify, the two ways you can look at multiple-year data is either by year to year, or you can look at it by class. To see an example of reviewing a multiple-year data set, watch the video at **bit.ly/2nddataset**.

Hopefully, this now gives you a better understanding of the second data set that you may receive, and the question may ask you to choose three concerns the data gives you about the school, teaching practices, or students. You could also be asked that once you have identified your areas of concern, to then provide solutions as to how you would fix these issues.

SUMMING UP

Now, having gone through two of the different types of data that you may come across on the test, you understand how to read these data sets, how to go through them, and how to identify concerns. Then, how to provide answers that the examiners are looking for.

The next chapter will also provide you with some "stock" answers to give you an even better idea of the kinds of answers you should produce for the constructed response part of the test.

Then, the chapter after that will look at forming your own study guide to study effectively for the day of the test.

20

STOCK ANSWERS (FOR ALL CONSTRUCTED RESPONSES)

*N*ow, having looked at how to deal with data in the constructed response part of the test, throughout the rest of this chapter, I will be showing you some "stock" answers that you could, in effect, apply to all questions you may be asked in this part of the test.

These are answers you can have in your back pocket in case you get stuck while writing your constructed response. They are not specific to the question and do not give the why so PLEASE do not ONLY use a stock answer. Of course, you will have to connect  the stock answer directly to the question to make it specific and

262 | DR. DESIREE ALEXANDER

give the why it is important. But again, these are some effective answers you can have in your armory to use at will.

Please carefully review the contents of this chapter and start applying them to your practice answers so that when it comes to the day of your test, you are well versed in how to produce ideal answers.

DUE PROCESS

What is due process? For example, if you have something going wrong with a teacher who got a complaint about them, or a student who got a complaint about them, or you observed something wrong, or whatever the situation is, you are going to go and talk to that person about the situation before you start doing any other steps. That is due process.

ALWAYS CLOSE THE COMMUNICATION LOOP

When somebody comes to you at the beginning, you need to talk to that same person at the end.

Let's say the superintendent brought you a complaint and told you to handle it. You're going to talk to that superintendent at the end of the process about how you handled the situation. That is an example of closing the communication loop.

Let's say a parent came to you with a complaint directly; no matter what happens, you are going to talk to that parent at the end. Whoever you talk to at the beginning, you will close that communication loop and talk to them at the end.

MEET WITH GROUPS SEPARATELY, AND THEN TOGETHER

Remember, any time you have any two or more groups that have complaints against each other, or any two or more people going against one another, you should talk to them separately and then together.

For example, parents and teacher met during the school year to create a science program; however, the parents started meeting just with the parents during the summer, and the teachers started meeting just with the teachers during the summer. Because the groups started meeting separately, two science programs were created with different criteria and the parents are upset with the teachers and vice versa. You're going to meet with each group separately first. You're going to meet with the parent group first. Then you're going to meet with the teacher group. Finally, you will bring both groups together. This would be a perfect time to re-establish the vision, mission and goals (why did we come together in the first place), but we will discuss that later.

STAKEHOLDER INPUT AND COLLABORATION ON EVERYTHING

As an educational leader, you make NO decisions on your own. You will get stakeholder input on every decision you make. Even when you want to go to the restroom, you ask your secretary if there is something you have to do or if you have time to go. That may be extreme, but it is truthful. Forming a committee is something you would do for any decisions that needs to be made. Now, on the test, because you want to be specific and say why, you will say WHO is on your committee, WHAT your committee is going to do, and WHY it is important to form that committee. The why may come from your data in the question or it may come from your knowledge that if you include others in your decision making, they can bring ideas and viewpoints you never thought of and they will have more buy-in (and implementation) because they had a hand in creating solutions.

ALWAYS LOOK AT THE DATA

As an educational leader, data influences everything you do, so you need to make this clear that you are always, always, always looking at the data.

Now, of course, we have already talked about you being specific. So, you are never going to just say as part of your answer that you would "look at the data" without telling them exactly *what* data.

Always mention that your go-to area for addressing any issues will be to look at the data, but always be specific. Some questions will give you data. For these, you want to take the different data points and use them together to answer your question. For example, if they give you test scores, a parent letter, and a teacher survey, don't just focus on one of these IF you are able to focus on more than one to back up your answer. If your answer is *we should focus on the teacher not teaching the curriculum,* I could write the parent letter saying the teacher watched movies all day, the teacher's test scores show that the report card grades are much better than the benchmark grades (which proves he is not teaching curriculum because the benchmark tests students' knowledge of the curriculum so who knows where those grades on the report cards are coming from), and the teacher survey shows the teacher reporting he does not know how to help his students. So all three data points prove your point. That is much stronger than using only one of them.

RE-ESTABLISH VISION, MISSION, AND GOALS

If you get a question where groups are going against each other (parents against teachers, paraprofessionals against teachers, etc.), you want to talk to the groups separately, and then bring them together. Whenever you are bringing a group back together, you are looking to get them back on the same page.

Your focus will be to re-establish why everyone is doing what they are doing. Remind them what their point for being there is. Re-establish your vision, mission, and goals.

PROFESSIONAL DEVELOPMENT

I feel like professional development is one of those answers that we do not use as much as we should. Just like using the data will be used many times, you should point to professional development more often than you may initially think.

Sometimes we only think about professional development as instructional professional development; however, it is more than this. It is not only about best practices and instruction.

If the teacher has a problem with coming to work on time, it could be about time management. Or, if your teacher is screaming every day and generally has anger issues, you could get some classroom management professional development, and you could also get some anger management alongside it. If your staff culture is just not there, then give some team-building professional development.

Professional development can really be for any situation. You can apply it to anything. You have just got to think about it outside of the box. Think of professional development as a form of training. Therefore, you can apply professional development to anything you would want to get training on.

ALWAYS GIVE A TIME AND A PURPOSE

Any time you mention that you are going to have your teachers collaborate or meet and work together, always give the timeframe and a purpose. So, if you say that you will have your teachers meet every week during their planning period to go through the test data, you have already provided the set time, and now all you need to do is write WHY this is important to do.

You need to make it clear when they will meet and why. The purpose could be something like grouping students by enrichment remediation. The time should be  when everyone is available. As an educational leader, you are responsible for scheduling this for your teachers.

CURRICULUM IS ALIGNED TO STATE NATIONAL AND STANDARDS

Any time that you write down "curriculum" as part of your answer, you must make sure that you state it must be aligned to the state and national standards. That is what curriculum mapping does, and aligning to the state and national standards makes it rigorous.

Common assessments are used to test whether your teachers are teaching a rigorous curriculum. For example, all of Ms. Smith's students are making A's and B's on their report cards, but this is because Ms. Smith is having her students color all day and assessing them on that; then you have Mr. Tom, and his students are making C's and D's on their report cards because they are struggling with the curriculum which is much tougher than what Ms. Smith is assessing her students on, then this is when that common assessment comes up. This is that assessment where everybody is going to take the exact same assessment, and the questions within it are aligned to the state and national standards. Sometimes these are called benchmarks when the school/district/state usually provides the test on the same time interval (like every quarter).

When that common assessment comes through, Ms. Smith's students are guaranteed to fail in this scenario. Because even though they are making A's and B's, they are doing that because they are coloring all day, which is easy to pass! Ms. Smith is not teaching a rigorous curriculum.

Where Mr. Tom's students may still make C's and D's, this would be because they are struggling with the curriculum. Nevertheless, you are able to compare Ms. Smith and Mr. Tom's students and how their report card grades differ or are the same as their common assessment grades. So, that is what common assessments are for, as they can show you who is doing what.

There may be an issue with who creates the common assessment and making sure what goes in it, but that is a whole different conversation. Nonetheless, you can state the purpose of using a common assessment. Therefore, if you are answering a question that deals with curriculum, you can include common assessments and also say why they are important.

PROGRESS MONITORING

Remember as an educational leader, you will always monitor the progress of any situation. This ensures that implemented solutions are producing positive outcomes.

Ways to progress monitor include things like observations and doing walkthroughs. Generally, you want to put across that you are keeping abreast of the situation, such as by having people meet with you to let you know what's going on with the situation.

SUMMARY

That brings us to the end of this chapter about stock answers. Hopefully, after reading through the chapter, you are getting a really good understanding of the mindset you need to be in during the constructed response part of the test.

Remember, these are stock answers that you can include if you get stuck about what ACTIONS to take. However, these will not help you if the question asks you to use the data to come to conclusions. These only help with taking ACTION, which some questions will ask you to do. Do not confuse this. You must understand what the question is actually asking you to do. We will discuss this more in the next chapter.

21

FORMING YOUR OWN STUDY PROGRAM

*T*his chapter will be useful for your practical study skills. The process started in this chapter will also be continued in the next chapter, which demonstrates how you can find a way to fit all topics into the four questions you have in the SLLA 6990 constructed response section.

The rest of this chapter provides some practical tips on creating a study guide that will ensure you are writing everything you need to provide as part of your answers in the constructed response part of the test.

CREATING YOUR OWN STUDY GUIDE

As I go through the process of showing you how to set up your study guide, I will show you the steps I would use, but I encourage you to add your own steps, too. Make your study guide personal to you.

Nevertheless, the best thing about this study guide is that we actually go through the different question types you'll come across in the constructed response part of your test, and then you create your answers based on that.

Then, study your answers. So that means that when you get to the test, you will be prepared and ready with thoughts about how to answer these questions based on the question type and the theme.

However, you need to remember that the key here is to make all your answers **specific**, and you also always must provide a **purpose/why**. You will know in what way you need to make your answer specific, as you can get this from the question. You can take the generic things that we come up with for your study guide and then connect them to the actual question to make them specific.

As described in earlier chapters, this means that instead of just saying you will put forward a committee, you are going to say something specific, such as you are going to form a committee of *X people*, which you will be able to extract from the question.

That is to say, the question is not going to tell you exactly who to put on the committee; that is your job to work out. But your skills here will tell you who you need to put on the committee; for example, it may be that you need some teachers, parents, community members, and so on.

So, the question is going to lead you to who you need on that committee. The question is going to tell you why forming a committee is important. Both of these will be your responsibility to state clearly in your answer, but the question itself will lead you to where you need to go with your answer.

MAKE GENERIC SPECIFIC

You may form a committee because it is important to give teachers space to use their voices, and you are asking them to be involved. But these are still generic answers. You need to seek the specific reason from the question.

Why would these generic reasons be important for this specific scenario? What specific reasons can you give that link forming a committee to the question? You need to take these generic things and find a way to connect them to the question.

Make your answer specific, and always mention *why* it is important. I cannot say this enough because this is how you pass this test. **The secret to passing: Making your answers SPECIFIC, telling WHY each answer is important, and**

making sure you are answering the ACTUAL question and ALL parts of the question!

THE DIFFERENT QUESTION TYPES AND THEMES

Let's go ahead and create our study guide. These are four types of questions you will encounter on the test:

A. Strategic Leadership (Student Engagement/Complaint)
B. Instructional Leadership (Instructional Improvement)
C. Climate and Culture Leadership (Diversity)
D. Ethical Leadership (Inclusivity)

Now, within these four questions, seven themes will continuously be mentioned/questioned: **complaints**, **curriculum**, **supporting teachers** (e.g., new teachers/bad teachers, and building a culture of support generally in the school), **supporting school board decisions**, **effectiveness of programs**, **community support**, and **interventions**.

Now, let's discuss the four types of questions.

Strategic Leadership

This question can be a complaint question. You may get a question about student engagement. For example, the teachers are only lecturing, the students are not engaged, and you, as the school leader, need to fix it. So they may ask what are three things the leader can do to help this situation. When you address it, you want to make sure that when you list something you will do, you back it up by saying WHY this is actually a problem, and HOW you know it is an issue (use the data they give you). Then, you can tell WHAT you would do and WHY you would do those things. That makes a perfect answer on this test. You MUST GIVE THE WHY and the HOW for everything you list on this test. You cannot just say this is how it is…how do you know that is how it is. You cannot just suggest something to do…why are you telling us to do this?

Instructional Leadership

This question will ask you about your leadership as an instructional leader. The question may pinpoint that your teacher is not teaching a rigorous curriculum (not teaching the standards). Your job would be to see how the data shows you the teacher is not teaching the curriculum and what you would do about it. For example, if the teacher's classroom grades are much higher than the students' scores on the benchmark tests, then that tells you that whatever the teacher is grading in the classroom is not on the same level as the benchmark tests, which will have questions based on standards. Well, if this is the case, you would write that the issue is the teacher not teaching the standards and HOW you know this to be true (the data and the explanation I gave above). Then you can discuss how to solve this issue (anything from providing PD to the teacher on how to read the curriculum and how to teach the curriculum, meeting with the teacher to provide help on letting the data drive instruction, and so forth).

Climate and Culture

This question will most likely be about diversity. It will ask how you ensure that your teachers provide an equitable environment for your diverse students. This can be with instruction, climate/culture, celebrations, inclusion, etc. Again, you will say what the issue is (according to the scenario and the data), how you know it is an issue (according to the data), how you correct it, and why those corrections are important. For this, you want to pinpoint what is being said and what is being done to make students feel less included. Usually, they will give you data that shows teachers are struggling with certain things (language barriers, change in demographics, teachers not being culturally relevant to new cultures in the school, teachers not teaching new culturally relevant curriculum, discipline skewed towards students of color, etc.). As with the other four, this question may or may not ask you how to fix the problem (action steps).

Ethical Leadership

This will be the question about are you an ethical leader, are you inclusive, and are you fair? This question may be about the treatment of groups of people on your campus. It may focus on racial diversity, sexual orientation, paraprofessional and support staff, etc. It will deal with how they are being treated and how they are being included (or not being included). It may be a question about clubs being formed or the treatment of support staff. You want to be sure to be technical in this question. No matter how people feel about the situation, what is the ***right and legal*** thing to do? This may be your most difficult question because it does not matter how you feel about the situation; it is about the ethical way to handle this fairly. Just as with the other three question types, you would include what the issue is and how you know it is an issue using the data provided for you. Then, if asked, you would list how you would solve this issue and why each of the ways you would solve it is important.

SENTENCE STARTERS

Before we move to the seven themes, let's discuss sentence starters.

You can see throughout the discussion of the four question types, you must be specific and tell how/why. Well, to help you with this and to help you answer every part of the question, you can use sentence starters.

For example, if the first question asks you to look at the data and tell three areas for improvement, and the second question asks you for each area of improvement and to tell how you would improve it, these would be my sentence starters:

The first area of improvement is...

This is because the _____ data shows that...

The first action to improve this is to...

This is important because...

You would do each of these sentence starters three times to answer the question that asked for three (the second area of improvement, the second action, the third area of improvement, the third action). You can either list the three areas of improvement first and then the three actions (which is what I would do) OR you can list an area of improvement and then an action with it.

Notice that sentence starters must come in twos. Why? Because you have to give the answer and then give the answer to HOW you know that or WHY it is important. By using sentence starters, it not only helps you answer each part of the question, but it makes it easier on your grader to see your answers, understand them and move on.

Now, let's discuss the seven themes.

Complaints

This is a question that you are *definitely* going to get. This is a common issue for an educational leader to face, so the examiners will surely include a question with a complaint on the test. You are going to get somebody complaining about something.

Curriculum/Instructional Improvement

You are also *definitely* going to get a question about the curriculum or instructional improvement. The question will be something such as changing a curriculum that is not working, updating a curriculum, adding a curriculum, or something else similar to these examples, which deal with curriculum.

Supporting Teachers / Creating a Culture of Support

You are going to get questions that cover these areas as well. It may be different kinds of questions, but it is going to be about supporting teachers and other adults in your building, and maintaining a culture of support in your school. This may be considering equity, diversity, or the overall cohesiveness of your staff.

Supporting School Board Decisions

As an educational leader, it is important that you show that you support school board decisions, so they may ask you about this too. When a school board makes a decision, you have to support it. Even if the decision is not one that you agree with, you must support it, especially in front of your staff, community and stakeholders. So you may get a question where the school board makes an unpopular decision and ask you to support it to the community.

Effectiveness of a Program

You may get a question about how you can tell if a program is effective. It may give you multiple years of data and ask how you can tell if this program has been successful over a span of time. Or, it may ask you to look at test scores and such to see if a certain instructional program is effective.

Community Support and Interventions

You may get a question about how to gather community support, such as how you get the community to support your school.

You may get a question about interventions. These questions will ask things like how you bridge the gap for any student that you have. It will ask you what kind of interventions you can use to help your student.

EXAMPLES OF INFORMATION QUESTION TYPES

Some questions will not ask you to list steps or actions, but instead will ask you for *information*. So, you must switch your brain from a *step* mode to actually analyzing and giving information.

Here are some examples of the question types you may be presented with on the test:

282 | DR. DESIREE ALEXANDER

- **After analyzing the data, identify three problems that have meaning for the school's vision and goals.**
- **What are the three factors the leader should consider before creating a professional development plan for the year?**
- **Name three factors that present a problem to a leader when trying to implement a strong curriculum instructional program.**

Notice that these questions do not ask you for steps. As with one of the above examples, "after analyzing the data, identify three problems that have meaning for the school's vision and goals," they didn't tell you to solve the problems; they're not asking you for the steps to solve it. They just said, tell us the three problems. So, what you need to do is tell them the problem, and then tell them why that is a problem using their data and your knowledge about being a leader.

For example, let's assume that the vision and goals would be to bring up student achievement. In this case, you could identify that one of the problems they are going to have is bringing students on grade level because students in some sections are so far behind their grade equivalency.

One of the problems that you can identify is that the school is going to have a problem bringing students up to where they need to be, so they can be on level for the next school year, as this currently does not meet their vision and goals. So, notice that you do not need to give any steps on how to solve that.

The question asked you what their problems are, meaning that the goal is not being met. The problem is bringing students up to the grade level because they are so far behind. Of course, you would include HOW you know this using the data given. This is all you would need to state for this question, plus two other problems. You would need to provide the information, not the steps.

Let's look at some other examples where you also have to think differently. "What are three factors a leader should consider before creating a professional development plan for the year?" Your answers should primarily include **data**. You also need to state *why* this is important. You could say that the principal should consider student data because wherever the student data is low, that is the area where teachers need professional development, so they can help those students come up in those areas.

As mentioned previously, only answer the question that is in front of you. Do not pull any information from anywhere else or present any hypotheticals.

The question also did not ask for steps in how you would create a professional development plan for the year. What the question actually asked is what are three factors that a principal should consider.

These factors could be, as aforementioned, things like student data, as well as based on the needs and wants of the teacher. The latter is certainly a factor the leader should consider – what the teachers want to learn – and why.

Make sure that you are only answering the question that is put in front of you, and that means you may switch your brain so as to not give any steps, as is required in other question types.

Another example from above is, "Name three factors that present a problem to a leader when trying to implement a strong curriculum and instructional program." This problem could be teacher knowledge. If the teachers do not understand the lesson plan from the curriculum or best practices to use, that could be a problem. So, put this as your answer and state why it is a problem.

There is no need to state how you are going to solve the problem because that isn't asked in this question type. You need to put in your answer what the problem is and why it is a problem.

It's a problem because the teachers do not know how to read the curriculum, don't know how to plan lessons using the curriculum, and don't know how to teach the curriculum. This means that a strong curriculum in the instructional program is not being implemented.

These information question types are different from the steps question types which ask you to list steps/actions you would take to solve problems, which is where your stock answers will become useful. However, many questions ask you for both information and steps/actions to better or solve the information you listed.

Throughout answering these questions, do not forget to make your answer specific by referring to the question and writing HOW you know this information (by using the data) or WHY this is important (by using the data or your knowledge).

KNOWING WHAT TO EXPECT

Now that you have read the above different question types, you will know what to expect on the test.

If you remember from the logistics part of this book, these are the questions that will have those single screens. They will just have the question, then you type your answer out at the bottom. The other types of questions will give you data and the question. In this case, you will have tabs of data to go through while you type your answer in the little box on the right side of the screen under the question.

22

ANSWERING STEPS/ACTION
QUESTIONS PER THEME

*A*fter having read the previous chapter, you will know how to begin to set up your study plan. At this point, you are probably wondering how you can study if you don't know what is in the question.

That is a good point. For information type questions, the best thing you can do is understand the type of information that will be in the question and how to decipher and answer it, which we did in the previous chapter. However, for steps/action type questions, you can plan a little more.

In this chapter, we will look at some steps/actions we can use when answering questions per our seven themes. This is helpful because when you are asked for STEPS/ACTIONS, you can have these ready to go (very similar to stock answers—see how it all circles back).

Now, I must warn you. Remember these will not be specific (because we do not have the question) and we cannot give a sufficient why (because we do not have the question). So you can use some of these examples on the test, but your job would be to make them specific by connecting them to the question and telling me why they are important according to the specific situation in the question.

COMBINING THE THEMES

As mentioned above, it is possible for questions to combine the themes discussed in the last chapter (complaints, curriculum, supporting teachers / creating a culture of support, supporting school board decisions, the effectiveness of a program, community support, and interventions).

For example, you may get a complaint question about a school board decision. Or it may be a curriculum question that asks how implementing a new curriculum could change the culture of your school and how you would support teachers during the implementation.

You may get questions that cover single themes, or questions that gel them together.

Also, you may get a question that asks you to create goals. Goals are different from steps/actions. A goal is WHAT you want to accomplish from the actions you take. So be very careful that your goal is not a step or action.

For example, a goal would be to ensure all teachers feel included. The step/action would be to form a committee of teachers where their input is heard, valued and acted upon. Notice that there is no action in the goal itself. The goal is what we hope to accomplish by performing the action.

And, as always, no matter what is asked of you (information or steps/actions), **remember that each part of the plan you write needs a WHY that is important, and each action step you write needs a WHY is that important and/or HOW will that help. If it is a goal, tell me WHY is this goal important/why did you make this a goal. In other words, look at the data and tell me what the problem was, WHY it is a problem and how this led to the goal you choose. That tells me WHY your goal is important.**

In this chapter, let's go through the themes you could see on the test and how you can answer the steps/actions questions of these four constructed response questions.

COMPLAINT QUESTIONS

When you have a complaint question where someone is complaining about someone else, the first thing you are going to try to do is to talk to the complainer. If the question tells you that the complainer came straight to you, then this will not be your first step, as the question tells you you have already spoken to the complainer.

If your question tells you the complainer is anonymous, this again will not be your first step. If it says there was an anonymous complaint in a newspaper and your superintendent brought it to you, you are not going to become a detective and find who wrote it.

If it is anonymous, then you cannot talk to the complainer. However, if someone came to you and told you that they heard a certain person was complaining, then your first step will be to talk to the complainer.

The second step here (or the first step if you are not talking to the complainer first, because of the reasons above) is due process. You must go and talk to that person who was complained about.

As always, for each one of these steps, you need to be **specific**, and you need to state *why* each step is important.

As part of due process, you need to talk to the person who is being complained about. If it is a group, you need to talk to the group that was complained about. You need to let them know exactly what the complaint about them is.

Next, you want to create actions that make sense to the question. For example, this may be to perform some type of investigation, including observations, walkthroughs, forming a committee, or looking at data. It really depends on what the complaint is.

If the complaint is about how a teacher is teaching or how a teacher is treating students, then that is where you would apply those observations and walkthroughs.

If it is a complaint on the curriculum, a complaint on grading practices, or anything like that, then that is where you may want to form a committee. This is also where you would need to start looking at data, as you would need to find out what is happening with the curriculum, whether it is being taught correctly, and if the curriculum is aligned with state and national standards.

Whatever the action steps will be really depends on what the complaint is, but action steps need to be there.

To clarify, the first thing you would do is talk to the person (or people) who was complained if you can. The second thing is to give due process. Then, the next thing would be to provide your action steps, whatever those action steps need to be.

Next up, you are going to give some solution steps. Solution steps may be providing that person with professional development, going through the curriculum and changing it as needed, setting up meetings with that person on a continuous basis, continuing to do walkthroughs, and whatever makes sense with the question.

So notice, you will begin with talking to the person; then you move through to your action steps; then you have your solution steps.

Finally, you are going to include progress monitoring. As you would remember from previous chapters, always start with due process, then end with progress monitoring and closing the communication loop.

You need to make it clear how you're going to keep an eye on the situation, such as continue to do walkthroughs and observations and keep on looking at student test data to see if the curriculum is working.

Other continual actions you might adopt include having your teachers meet once a month during professional development day to review and assess the situation. Remember, for each step, you are also going to state why.

Finally, you should always close the communication loop. This means getting back to whoever brought you the problem in the beginning. If it is the complainer themselves, get back to the complainer. If somebody just brought you the complaint (perhaps the superintendent), then get back to the superintendent. If the board brought you the complaint, then get back to the board. Whoever brought you the complaint in this scenario, you need to get back to them again to close the loop.

Notice here that you have about six steps that you can take, and you may remember in a previous chapter, I said to only put three and move on. Sometimes this is difficult because you want to put more, but put three – put your top three, then move on. Come back and fill in some more afterward if you have time.

Remember some practical advice about creating your study guide. As with the above example, if you can think of any additional steps, include them. Write it down and keep these answers in the back of your mind.

Then, when it comes to taking your test, as soon as you walk in, you can start jotting things down, things that you remember from your study guide.

CURRICULUM QUESTIONS

Let's say for this question you have a problem with the curriculum. Somebody requests that you update the curriculum. Somebody requests that you change the curriculum. What are you going to do? And I must remind you, this advice is ONLY for the steps/actions type of questions...not for questions that ask you for information (as we discussed earlier).

Step one could be to form a committee. You do not want to be the only person solving any issue (except for possibly a complaint since you need to be confidential). From the question, you would include who should be on this committee, what the committee will do, and why it is important to form a committee.

Now that you have your committee, it is feasible that the committee would meet to review your curriculum to see if it is rigorous. In other words, you are going to do curriculum mapping. Your answers do not have to be on the stock answer list, but you are going to review the curriculum to make sure the curriculum is part of the state/national standards.

If someone has asked you to renew the curriculum or change the curriculum, then the first thing you need to know is what curriculum is being used now; then, you will want to look at the data. You need to evaluate what your student data tells you about this curriculum. If someone has asked you to change the curriculum, and the student data says they are learning from it, why are you changing it?

To clarify, your first step is to form a committee, and then do the rest of the steps, which are to review the current curriculum to see if it is rigorous.

Step three could be to analyze student data. You are going to look at that student data, but again you need to be specific about what data you are looking at. For example, it might be student test scores or student grades in the classroom. By looking at the student data, it will indicate what you need to do next.

Then, since you are implementing a program, you can compare it to similar schools. What you want to know is how similar schools implemented this new curriculum. Did they implement it well? What mistakes did they make? You can learn from their experiences and not fall into the same mistakes. You can also look at their successes. You can find out how much it helped their students.

Then, once your research is done, whenever you decide to actually implement it, the next step you'd need to provide is giving your teachers some professional development. Naturally, you need to train them on the changes to the curriculum.

You would provide them with two separate professional developments. One would be on how to read the curriculum and lesson plan from it, and the other would be on best practices to teach the curriculum. You would give them continuous professional development. Remember the same best practices you learned in the multiple choice section can and should be used in the constructed response section.

Now you want to progress monitor the implementation of the curriculum with your teachers and committee. This may involve having your teachers collaborate, such as having your teachers meet every week during their planning period to look at the data, review student work, see where the curriculum needs to be modified, and see how it is being taught. Overall, you are looking to see how successful you have been with implementation of the curriculum. If it is not successful, find out why, and you may need to modify the curriculum or how it is being taught.

The main thing to remember, as with everything else on the test, is to make your points **specific** and always give reasons *why*. Do not be afraid of repeating yourself from question to question. And definitely use your study guide to maximum effect!

You can see from the example of this type of question how, as part of your answer, you are combining different elements, such as including stakeholder input, reading data, thinking about the culture, and getting your teachers to have professional growth.

Answering with specificity and giving the reason why your answer is important shows that you understand the question, and you are answering in a way that explains how you'd deal with the scenario.

CULTURE OF SUPPORT QUESTIONS

A question on the test may ask you how you support your teachers and how you support your culture. So think about teachers in general. What do educators want in order to feel supported? What are best practices?

The first thing I am going to say is form a committee. Forming a committee in this regard allows you to ask the people you are trying to motivate how they want to be motivated. You can ask them what help they need and how you can provide that. You can ask them how you can help them do their jobs better.

Next, look at the data. Remember that data is not only test scores. It is not only student data. You could create data by sending out a survey to your teachers to ask them what they want to learn and satisfaction surveys. Then the committee can look at that data.

If there is nothing mentioned in the question about data, you can mention that you will create data. You could state that you are going to create a survey, send it out, and then that will be the data you analyze to see how the teachers can be better supported.

Next, you are going to take some action steps. What are some ways that you support teachers? Give your teachers collaboration time to look at content and what they are doing in the classroom and instruction, and give them collaboration time for team building. Give them collaboration time to meet and support each other with those in their professional learning network.

Instead of only using the collaboration time to go through the data or something very specific, also give the teachers some time when they can come together and talk about concerns, which means they can get help with situations they are dealing with. This is especially the case with new teachers, as they need more support.

Some other kinds of support you can give to your teachers is to provide mentor teachers. This is something that even veteran teachers can benefit from. You may not call them mentors, but that is essentially their role. You could call them mentors or refer to them as buddy teachers.

Other actions to take include providing them observation time, when they can go and observe other teachers and see what they are doing in their classroom. You could provide them guidance and teach them how to self-reflect by reviewing their own teaching practices and making changes according to what they see.

For example, they can record their own teaching to see what they are actually doing and the impact they are making. Show them how to self-journal, allowing them an opportunity to comment on the things that they need to work on. This is self-reflective processing.

You could also do book studies, where you are encouraging your teachers to learn about different things. Additionally, you could start giving them leadership roles to start building them up.

Always give them professional development and give them opportunities for growth. Send them to workshops. Send them to conferences. See what they want to learn and help them in that learning. Help them grow.

Basically, mention all those things that you would want as a teacher to feel supported. You could provide them a designated time every month to meet with you, and that's their time to bring concerns.

These are the kinds of action steps that I would do to support teachers or build a support culture. Building your culture is making sure your teachers feel supported and feel like they are actually making a positive difference on your campus.

You can always finish your steps for teacher support with progress monitoring. This means keeping an eye on how your teachers are feeling.

Again, that could be with surveys. Or that could be with meetings or other actions such as walkthroughs and observations. Whatever you need to do to keep your eye on how your teachers feel.

When you are dealing with the culture of the school, you need to bring students into it as well. If you are dealing with a cultural question, then you need to bring in how your students are feeling, too

Put some students on that committee as well. Do a student survey also. Monitor the progress of the students. Take action steps for the students, such as an incentive program where you reward positive behavior, for example.

When thinking about the culture of the school, these are the things you could add to all of the teacher support steps already mentioned. You could include assemblies and pep rallies. You could do honors programs or anything that just supports your students and helps appreciate their identity in the school.

For example, you could have a student-only committee to get ideas of what the students need. You could also start a student government so that they can have some autonomy. It is the little things that sometimes go unrecognized that impact the culture of your school, and those should be part of your action steps.

What do you do with new teachers or bad teachers? Actually, it is mostly the same actions that you can take. Give them a mentor, let them observe, or do observations and provide feedback in meetings with you. It can be all the same actions as providing any support because, essentially, you need to help them try to become better teachers. You will have them meet with you for support.

SUPPORTING SCHOOL BOARD DECISIONS

You may get a question about supporting school board decisions.

First, you might get a question about the school board making a decision, and the community is upset with it, and they have asked you to handle it.

For example, it is requested that you put together a presentation to show the school board or your community that demonstrates why you support this decision.

The other type of question about the presentation becomes an information question because they may ask you what you need to put in the presentation and who you need to get that from. We are going to look at both.

Let's look at the step question first that asks you to get the community on your the side of the decision.

First, have a faculty meeting to inform your staff of the school board decision and how they need to communicate about it if they are asked about it. You can tell them what your talking points are and also provide other instructions, such as not talking to the media.

This depends on the scenario, but the first step may be to set up your faculty for success. Then, form a committee. Depending on the scenario, you may not do the faculty meeting first; you may just form a committee. Nevertheless, you always need to reach a point where you form a committee to come up with the steps on how you are going to get the community on board.

Gather the data to see what the actual decision was and why it was made. You will need to know exactly the ins and outs because as soon as this decision is released into the community, they will ask questions. They are going to know their data, and so you must get your data on why this decision was made.

You should also find out how the decision is going to help your campus and how this decision is going to help your district, as these are the things that the community is going to want to know. It is vital that you get your data and get it straight.

From here, there are even more action steps you can take. This may include a community forum or a town hall meeting where you invite the community and the parents to discuss the decision. A forum such as this gives you the opportunity to tell them exactly what the decision was and why it was made.

You may need to have more than one meeting so that people from the community can come at different times that suit them, but it shows you are doing your best to reach them all and not leaving anyone behind and disgruntled because they feel like they have been left out of the loop.

Then, you can form a passive communication plan for those people that cannot come to the in-person meeting. Even though you have made the meetings as accessible as possible, you are still doing your best to make sure that people in the community are still getting the information even if they cannot come to meetings.

Some parts of your passive communication plan will be to create pages on a website where you can display information. Or you can make calls to your parents using an automated system.

You can send home flyers or newsletters. Those are all passive ways to communicate, and you need to do that because not everybody can come to the in-person meetings, but you still want them to get the information.

You also want to have some kind of way for parents and the community to communicate with you. For example, you could request their feedback via a survey, or you could welcome any responses via a dedicated email address that is set up.

If you say that you are going to create an online forum, where people can come together and discuss, you need to say that it is a moderated forum. In other words, your committee must be the ones to approve the comments. Otherwise, giving it free rein can get a little bit out of control.

If you are going to talk about going to the media, you need to get superintendent approval. This could be if you intend on going on the local morning news program or if you are going to write a letter to the editor of the local newspaper.

Those are some of the action steps. As you can see, some are active actions, and some are passive. You could include all your active actions in one bullet and all your passive actions in another. That would be two separate steps.

Then, of course, you are going to progress monitor the situation. Just because you have taken your action steps, you don't want to assume everything is OK, or bask in ignorance and then realize later that people are planning a protest you didn't know about.

You want to keep an eye on the situation and keep your communication consistent with the community.

Also, get them to communicate with you and continually meet with the committee so you can know what is going on. Make sure there are some parents and community members on that committee too. They will be the ones you can check in with. You need to get everyone on the same page, and that is how you're going to handle the step question.

Now, if you get an information type of question like one that asks you to do a presentation in front of a committee, what you should include in the presentation, and where you get that from, this strictly depends on what the scenario is.

However, for example, let's say that it is about cutting recess. In this example, the district has said they will cut recess, and now they want you to promote this in the community. The question asks you what some of the things that you are going to need are.

If it is about cutting recess, and you are supposed to support it, even if you agree or not, the first thing is you will need to look at things like the bell schedule, so you will need to know where you can get the bell schedule. Let's just say you could ask the school secretary for that.

Now that you have the bell schedule, look at it to reveal where those instructional minutes are going if recess is cut. As an example of something positive, you could identify that you can dedicate more time to reading.

You can also look at student test scores to identify areas that need improvement. Then you could suggest that the minutes cut from recess could be put into areas that need improvement, such as extra instructional minutes or tutoring in science. The test scores could be obtained from the campus test administrator, district test administrator, or coordinator. Or, you could get it from your state education website.

You can do other things like consult your PE teacher about doing that physical activity that they would do during recess during PE class instead. Other actions you can take include things such as doing research from similar schools that have cut recess, and then had their test scores go up. You can get those scores and information from websites.

Do not overthink it. You must come up with a plan, and you need to put it into a presentation and state where you got the information from.

EFFECTIVENESS OF A PROGRAM QUESTIONS

We already know from multiple choice that any time you want to see if anything is effective, you are going to look at student data. But you need to state how exactly this shows that a program is effective.

The questions you get on the test may ask you something about how you monitor a program over multiple years. So, how would you know if a program is effective?

306 | DR. DESIREE ALEXANDER

Number one, of course – and here it is again – you will form a committee. Number two, of course – and once again, here it is – you are going to look at the data. This time it is student data to see if this program is effective. Also, remember that you must be specific in your answer.

Do these two things first, and then do observations and walkthroughs, and other activities to see the program in action. You want to see, or rather you want to at least keep an eye on, what is happening with the implementation of the program. You may need to get some professional development for your teachers on the program to ensure that the program is being implemented effectively and that they are modifying it wherever it is needed to be successful.

You are going to do walkthroughs, observations, and continuously analyze data to progress monitor the implementation of the program. That is how you know what is *actually* being done versus what you say *should* be done.

You must make sure that your teachers have collaboration time to continuously look at the data. You need them to meet every week to view the data. You want them to see if the program is being as effective as you want it to be.

If the question asks you how you monitor a program over multiple years, you can do that in three ways. You can either monitor the program by grade level, monitor the program by class, or do both.

As mentioned before, if you monitor the program by grade level, then you would analyze what is your student data for fifth grade in 2017, then what is your student data for fifth grade in 2018, and how it compares. You can ask what changed in fifth grade from one year to the next if you see any huge changes in data.

You could also monitor the program over the same class. You could ask, "When the fifth graders were in fifth grade, how did this program affect them? And then when they went to sixth grade, how did this program affect them?" You can monitor it by grade level, so fifth grade for one year versus fifth grade from another year. Or you can do it by class, such as asking how the class of 2020 dealt with this program in the fifth grade, how they dealt with it in the sixth grade, or how they dealt with it in the seventh grade.

Those are ways that you monitor a program over multiple years. Notice that it was all about student data. Any time you want to know if a program is effective, you must refer to student data. Remember that data is not just test scores; it could include information from things like satisfaction surveys or interviews.

COMMUNITY SUPPORT

Any question you get on the test about community support is essentially going to ask you how you get the community to actually support your school. Here is how you can go about answering this.

In the first step, you can form a committee that includes community members and businesses. You are going to do this to see how to get the community to support you and then do the required steps for this to happen.

For the second step, you can invite your community to events on your campus. For example, when you are having the honor ceremony, you're going to invite them to it.

The third step is one that we often do not think about. You can invite your community to be active on your campus. In addition to inviting them to special events, invite them to participate actively on your campus, like coming to read to your students or come to teach a lesson. You could ask community members to be part of career day or similar event where they can tell students about their businesses or about what they do.

Another thing people often do not think of when it comes to community support is to ask them how they can be supported. Ask them what they need and what your school can do to help. For example, that could be a food drive, going to pick up trash, and some other volunteer activity supporting the community.

You need to show the community that support is not one-sided, as you are also asking the community how you can support them. You want to know how you can support your community as a school. In real life, this is especially important if you do not live in the community where you work.

Let your students and parents see you go to places and do things in the community, even if this is just letting them see you out shopping. Or attend community events, like the local county fair. Allow them to see you in the community doing normal things.

Last of all, of course, you will end with the progress monitoring. You are going to make sure that the committee keeps up with who you are supporting and how you are supporting them. You need to talk about how many times you are reaching out, how you are reaching out, and when you are reaching out to ensure the community feels supported and feels like they are a part of your school community to support you. You can even do surveys and interviews as progress monitoring tools.

INTERVENTIONS

This theme is all about asking how you support your students. Questions may ask certain things like, "Johnny is a new student at your school. Johnny is supposed to be going to the fourth grade. Johnny's mother comes to you and says she doesn't feel like he's ready for the fourth grade."

How do you promote Johnny to the fourth grade and still bridge the gap of him not having all the skills from third grade?

Think about how you might answer this. How do you support any student who is not on grade level?

The first step is to form a committee. This should include the student, the parent, the teacher from the third grade, the teacher from the fourth grade and you – the school leader. They are all going to be on a committee because they need to support this student alongside you.

Then, you are going to look at the data. Look at the test scores and any other relevant data so you can build your action plan. You might want to ask questions about the maturity of the student. You will want to observe the student during school (class, lunch, recess) to see if the student is getting along with others and handling the content (including the academics and social aspects).

In your action plan, you want to come up with ways to help Johnny. That could be by giving Johnny tutoring before school, after school, during lunch, or whenever. You are providing Johnny tutoring to get him up to grade level. You want to put Johnny in a program where the skills that he is missing from third grade can be taught, like a remediation program.

You want to give Johnny's parents some training on how they can help at home. Together, you are building some of these skills that Johnny does not have.

You may do some double-blocking where Johnny is in third-grade math and fourth-grade math to try to build those skills. These are interventions you would put into place to help that student come back and upgrade those skills they do not have.

You also want to give your teachers some collaboration time. You want those third- and fourth-grade teachers to have some special collaboration time just to talk about those students who may be in that double-blocking intervention situation.

Give them some time to meet so they can discuss how to better deal with Johnny and how to better help him. You want to make sure that the committee meets at certain times because you want to get everybody on track, including the student.

You want to let Johnny know how he is doing, and you can tell him, "This is where we are, and this is where we need to be." All those kinds of things are part of your action steps.

So, those would be your action steps, and then you are going to progress monitor. Some of the things you are already doing in your action steps can be done as progress monitoring, such as observations and walkthroughs to see Johnny in action, how he is dealing with whatever is happening, and how he is progressing.

Make sure that teachers are talking about the data on a continuous basis. Make sure that you are doing walkthroughs and observations. Anything that involves keeping track of how Johnny is doing is part of your progress monitoring. Keep track of what is working and what needs to change. Those are all part of your progress monitoring steps.

SUMMARY: COMBINING THEMES TO FIT FOUR QUESTIONS

We have now reached the end of this chapter which is about how to use all the different themes to answer the four questions in the constructed response.

In this chapter, we have gone through the seven different themes of questions that will run throughout the four questions in the constructed response section of the test (which you were introduced to in the last chapter). As a reminder, those seven themes are complaints, curriculum, culture of support, supporting decisions, effectiveness of programs, community support, and interventions.

Many of the questions combine two or more of these themes and combine step questions with information questions. If you follow the guidelines presented to you in this chapter, and you have formed your own study guide as was recommended in the last chapter, then you should be able to gain high scores for the constructed response part of the test.

Coming up next is the final chapter in this part of the book and the book's final chapter overall. By now, you should have a really excellent grasp of just what is required to pass the SLLA 6990 test, both the multiple choice section and the constructed response section.

When you feel confident that you have learned everything in this chapter, move on to the next and final chapter, which discusses leadership styles.

23

WRAPPING UP CONSTRUCTED RESPONSE: THE FOUR QUESTION TYPES

Congratulations on reaching the final chapter of the book! This chapter has been designed to round off your knowledge and prepare you for the four question types in the constructed response section.

These were already featured in Chapter Twenty, but here, in this chapter, we will discuss them a little deeper.

As with the previous ends of each part of the book, this chapter also includes a "thinking activity" for you to try at the end. Completing the activity will help you wrap up everything discussed as part of your preparation for the constructed response section of the test.

After that, it is hoped that you will be well and truly prepared to take the SLLA 6990!

BUILDING ON YOUR STUDY GUIDE

In the last chapters, you started your study guide. Revise and add to your study guide as you think of new answers or themes. When you get to the test, after you have studied your study guide, you will be able to have all these answers in the back of your brain.

After you read the question, new answers are going to come up, but you will still have all those answers that you already came up with. This means that you are bound to be well-prepared for the test.

When you get to the test, you will read each question to see which one of the question types it falls in to (we will discuss the four question types more in this chapter). You will also be able to see if the question(s) is an information question or a steps/action question and answer accordingly. You may also notice one or more of the seven themes in the question. Because we have discussed ways to answer all of these different questions, you will be more prepared to answer them successfully. But remember, you have to actually practice and study to be prepared. You also just need to make your answers specific and relevant to the question and explain HOW you know the answer (information question—use data from the question) or WHY your answer is important (steps question—use your knowledge or best practices).

Now, let's continue to build your study guide. These are four types of questions you will encounter on the test:

A. Strategic Leadership (Student Engagement/Complaint)

B. Instructional Leadership (Instructional Improvement)

C. Climate and Culture Leadership (Diversity)

D. Ethical Leadership (Inclusivity)

Let's take a deeper dive into each one.

STRATEGIC LEADERSHIP

This question can cover anything dealing with achieving goals through your leadership. Many times, this question uses the complaint theme. You may get a question about student engagement, where parents and teachers complain that certain teachers on campus are just doing lectures and not engaging the students or not teaching with the approved curriculums/programs. The question may ask, "What are three steps to handle this situation?"

There are different action steps you can take and different ways to approach it if you really think about it for what it is, which is a complaint-themed question and a step question.

318 | DR. DESIREE ALEXANDER

So some steps may be to meet with the parents to see what their complaint really is about, looking at teacher and student data to see if the complaint is valid, doing observations to see if the complaint is valid, and talking to students to see if the complaint is valid. Of course, you must complete due process to tell the teacher that a complaint was made against them. All of these will be involved if the question is as above.

However, if you are asked for a three-step strategy to ensure that teachers are engaging, that becomes a more instructional leadership question. It still fits, however, into strategic leadership because you are going to create a strategy to make sure that your teachers are actually engaging their students.

To answer this, you want to consider whether you are meeting with your teachers to see what they perceive about their classrooms. Do they perceive that students are engaged? What do they think about their classroom? Maybe they know that engagement (or whatever the question is about) is not a strength of theirs, and they want help.

You are mainly meeting with the teachers to see what their perceptions on their classrooms are, and then you can investigate how you can help them to be more engaging.

Therefore, one of your steps could be to get them professional development on student engagement, or practical hands-on instruction.

They can observe other teachers in their same grade level and content to see how they can be more engaging; this is how they could have taken the lesson and done it differently, or whatever the situation is, or whatever the scenario may be.

During this process, you are going to do some classroom observations, evaluations, and walkthroughs, and you are going to talk to students. While the teachers are doing these activities and implementing strategies to make the class more engaging, you need to make sure that all of these ideas are actually working. As part of your progress monitoring, you are then going to come back together with the teachers. This is going to be a process of asking whether it is working or not working. Also, look at the student data, which is going to be the student test scores and the students' comments from their surveys, which ask if the class is more engaging.

With that type of question, you want to make sure you understand what it is really asking you. Is it asking you to handle the complaint, or is it asking you to fix the problem (in this case, engagement)? You cannot answer a question successfully until you realize what is actually being asked of you!

INSTRUCTIONAL LEADERSHIP

An instructional leadership question will ask you about improving instruction in some way. It may give you some test scores (and we have already gone through this extensively) and ask you what needs to be improved.

Not only what, but how can it be improved? What actions can lead to improvement?

This is nothing new; the scenario will be something like you are given test scores and asked what you can do to improve instruction. These ideas have already been covered in previous chapters.

However, one thing to note is the difference between curriculum, instruction and assessment. Of course, all three go together to create a strong instructional program. But a teacher may have a problem with one and not the other. For example, Mr. Smith may have a problem teaching the curriculum. You can tell this by his report card grades being much better than his benchmark or end of course grades. If he were teaching the curriculum daily, then his report card grades would be similar to his benchmark grades.

Mr. Smith may have a problem with instruction. This means he is not engaging his students into his lessons and his lessons may lack purpose or depth. Are they watching videos every day that have nothing to do with content? How is he instructing his students and what are they actually doing?

Mr. Smith may also have a problem with assessments. This is shown by the type of assessments he chooses for his students. For example, he may not include open-ended questions, common assessments, projects, and essays in his class.

Notice that Mr. Smith may be strong in one of these areas, but weak in another. So, on the test, you may need to pinpoint which of these is the concern (or it may be all three, but you now know how to separate them into three separate areas of concern).

CLIMATE AND CULTURE LEADERSHIP

This question type could be something dealing with diversity. It could take the form of a question where you get different types of feedback (teacher or student surveys or interviews, or leader observations) about the culture of your school.

The scenario will usually show concerns of populations (students, teachers, parents, paraprofessionals, etc.) not feeling included or feeling discriminated against. For example, your Hispanic or African American students get stricter punishments. Or maybe teachers are even making remarks that your underrepresented students are not up to par.

322 | DR. DESIREE ALEXANDER

If the question is giving you this information, then you have a cultural problem. They want you to understand that you have a cultural problem that everybody is feeling.

The teachers are saying it; the students are saying it. It is not just that somebody perceives something; it is actually there, not just a perception. You are seeing it from all sides, or you are hearing it from half or over half of your teachers and/or students.

The question may ask you what the leader can do to change the culture. If you really think about it, that is a pretty generic question for such a high-level scenario. What they are trying to see in this question is not only can you answer the question, but can you take the emotions out of your decision-making.

This should anger you. This should make you upset that a teacher is saying that your underrepresented or minority students are lesser. You know that your teachers are not striving to help those students. They have already given up on those students. That should anger you; that should make you upset.

However, when you are making decisions as an educational leader, you have to take those emotions out of your decision-making. They want to see how you will answer a rather emotionally charged question.

The first thing you would do to change this culture is what you would do to change any culture, and that is forming a committee of teachers and students. The committee would be tasked with getting to the root of the issue and creating action steps to bettering the culture.

It is about bringing those people together to create situations and create space where teachers can check their own biases. Is there any bias towards certain groups of students?

Another step you would take is to provide some professional development for teachers on cultural sensitivity, cultural responsiveness, engagement, and equity. All of those things create your culture and your climate. This means that as a leader, you can start determining who is not on board. It will become obvious. However, it doesn't mean to give up on those educators. Becoming more culturally aware is a journey and a process.

But, you are trying to change something. Everyone is working towards making it better, and if certain people are not on board with that after a certain amount of time, you do not need them at the school. All those things are steps to create that change and create that culture. Sometimes you will have to lose people.

You need some students on that committee. You want your students to know that they did not just fill out a survey to say that the school has created inequity in their punishments, and then nothing happened. You either need students on that committee, or you could form a separate student committee that will meet with the leaders. You need to know how bad things are and how you can do better.

Feedback from these committees should be collected and used to determine next steps/strategies to improve school culture in a specific amount of time.

As always, you want to make your answer specific. Even though they gave you an emotionally charged scenario, and then the question is pretty basic, you can still answer in a specific way. The question here is how you *change* culture for the better.

ETHICAL LEADERSHIP

Last, but not least, is ethical leadership. You are going to get a question that tests your ethics and asks you about how you are inclusive. They want to know if you are *fair*.

For this kind of question, you may get a question about clubs. It may be about the inclusion of a certain club. It may be a diversity, religious or sexual orientation club, for example.

The question could ask something about a club being formed, and teachers are against it. The teachers do not feel like it should be on the campus. Parents speak out against this. The students speak out against it. What do you do? The question could also ask you about any population on your campus being treated unfairly (paraprofessionals, support staff, students, etc.). If that happens, what do you do?

Any kind of ethical leadership question is going to present you with some type of ethical dilemma. As an educational leader, you must be fair and ethical in all decision-making. Whether that goes against your personal beliefs or not, you have to be ethical and fair, nonetheless.

This is what the question is trying to find out. They want to know if you understand the ethical considerations and that you know how to have those difficult conversations, when necessary, be they with teachers, parents, or other stakeholders.

The question being asked is making sure that you have an inclusive campus and that you're being fair and ethical.

FINAL THOUGHTS ON CONSTRUCTED RESPONSE

Remember that this entire section of the book makes up your study guide for constructed response. But in order for it to be successful, you must actually study it.

Once more, any answer you provide on the test must be specific, and you must state how you know that answer or why that answer is important. You cannot simply write generic answers.

You can get the specifics from the question. Every question has a specific scenario to answer. This scenario is going to tell you who you need on that committee and what data you need, for example.

As for the "how," you cannot just say what you think for those information questions. You have to say what you conclude, but must tell HOW you know this from the data that is presented.

Remember those sentence starters come in twos: *This is the concern* AND *this is the concern because…*

As for the "why," that will always depend on your scenario too. What you are answering is *why* anything you do is **important**, and this means applying your answer to the *scenario* in the question. For those steps/actions questions, the why (from your knowledge of best practices) is crucial. Remember those sentence starters come in twos as well: *The first action is* AND *this action is important because…*

This is now the end of the constructed response part of this book, and aside from the afterword that follows this chapter, it is also the final chapter in this book. Throughout this part of the book, we have looked at all the different question types and themes that you are likely to see in the SLLA 6990 constructed response section. You have also built a study guide to prepare you for the test day.

There is a final thinking activity below. It is recommended that you complete this to enhance your understanding of what was covered in this part of the book regarding the constructed response section. After completing that, you should be truly prepared for your test.

All that's left for me to say is, *GOOD LUCK*!

THINKING ACTIVITY:

As you begin to practice constructed response questions and take practice tests, write down some common themes you see in the four different types of constructed response scenarios/questions.

For example, what are some common points they want you to consider on equity questions? (Do students feel they belong? Do teachers feel differently about their students since the population changed, such as students are not as invested/smart as they were before? Are all students being motivated/promoted/honored? etc.).

You will start noticing patterns in each of the four types of questions. Once you notice patterns, start considering how you will respond to these patterns.

Write down the pattern and your response to the pattern in your own study guide.

You can find more resources here: www.educatoralexander.com/slla-test-prep

AFTERWORD

...WHAT NOW?

Now that you have read this book and have used it as a resource in your studies, it is time for you to create your study plan. How many days do you want to study and for how many hours a day?

Be very honest with yourself and be mindful of your schedule. Question what you can realistically achieve as you create this plan. Remember to take time to rest and step away from the material, too, as this helps you process.

Just note, that there is no perfect way to study. Every person is different, so decide what is best for you and then go ahead with your personalized plan. YOU GOT THIS!

Remember to register for the test and give yourself time to prepare for the actual test-taking day as well. Are you taking it at a test center? Are you taking it at home (if that is still an option)? Prepare yourself mentally and physically for test day!

Gather all the resources you need, make sure you know where the testing center is, and decide what to wear to ensure you are comfortable.

Decide what else – if anything – you will be doing on the actual testing day, and prepare yourself for this, no matter how big or small, or how trivial any of it seems. Prepare yourself for all of it.

A final tip is that you may want to think about taking the day off from work or anything that might aggravate or upset you on the day you take the test. Also, consider your own body clock and biorhythms.

If you are a morning person, take the test in the morning. If you need time to wake up to become your best self, take it in the afternoon. You know what is best for you, and book your test around your best self.

I have no doubt you will be successful on this journey. Remember the other resources you have access to at educatoralexander.com/slla-test-prep.

Take care of yourself, study, do your best, and control what you can control. You will conquer this standardized test!

You are ready! Good luck!

ACKNOWLEDGMENTS

One of the best things that happened to me was finding *Words Will Win* copy editing service. There is no way I could have completed this book without the advice from George Perry! I had no idea where to start or what to do. He took my work and molded it into the book you see today!

I must give tremendous thanks to Bridgette Fortenberry for reading the book before all others (and over and over again) to give edits and valuable feedback. I also have to thank two Fiverr Level 2 Sellers*: ebookcover_xper* for creating my book covers and *evanego* for transcribing my online classes to help create the content for this book. In addition, my thanks go to Lisa S. Lloyd for transcribing an earlier version of this book starting the entire process years ago. Thank you to EduMatch Publishing and Dr. Sarah Thomas for believing in this book and publishing it. I would like to thank all my family and friends for supporting me during this process (and through life in general). Finally, I would like to thank all my family and friends for supporting me during this process (and through life in general), especially my mother, Francheska Pellerin Alexander (my daily rock) and my father, Clement D. Alexander, Sr. Without them, NONE of this would be possible.

Without this dream team, this book would still be on my to-do list. Thanks so much to all of you.

ABOUT THE AUTHOR

Dr. Desiree Alexander is an award-winning, multi-degreed educator who has been in the educational field since 2002. She is the Founder and CEO of **Educator Alexander Consulting, LLC** and the Deputy Director for the Associated Professional Educators of Louisiana. She consults with members of several schools/businesses and presents at conferences globally.

Dr. Alexander is lifetime certified in Louisiana in Secondary English Education, as a Reading Specialist, as a School Librarian, as an Educational Technology Facilitator, as an Educational Technology Leader, and in Educational Leadership.

She is certified in Texas as a Principal, in English Language Arts and Reading for grades 4-8 and grades 8-12, as a Reading Specialist for grades EC-12, and as a School Librarian.

She holds multiple technology certifications, and her company is a Google Partner with Education Specialization.

She holds a Bachelor's, a Master's + 30, and an Education Specialist Degree in Curriculum and Instruction from Louisiana

State University, a Master of Library Science from Texas Woman's University, and a Master of Educational Leadership with a concentration in Educational Technology Leadership from Nicholls State University. She also holds a Doctorate in Education with a concentration in Educational Leadership from Lamar University.

Learn more at www.educatoralexander.com.

www.ingramcontent.com/pod-product-compliance
Lightning Source LLC
Chambersburg PA
CBHW061135120626
46546CB00005B/1799

* 9 781953 852892 *